Publisher

This book has been published in collaboration with Create Space. It is also available through Amazon Kindle and Smashwords or on Dr. Cha~zay's website, www.corefreedom.com.

Book Version & Updates

Current Version: 1
First Published: May 22, 2015
ISBN Number-13: 978-1511813532
ISBN Number-10: 1511813539

To receive updates of new course and new book releases, visit http://corefreedom.com to get a free gift and subscribe to Dr. Cha~zay's newsletter.

Legal Disclaimer

The author is not a licensed medical practitioner, medical doctor, psychiatrist or psycho-therapist. She is a Metaphysician, certified Hypnotist, Reiki Master and Certified Grief and Suicide Hotline Counselor. If you are concerned about your own or anyone else's mental stability, please consult a professional. If you are suicidal, call 1-800-SUICIDE (within the United States). If you are elsewhere, please reach out to someone. Everything in this book reflects the author's personal journey as an individual, and reflects her own vision, experiences and her research into this topic through the interaction with her clients.

Rights and Copyright

Subliminal Messages

This book has been sprinkled throughout with subliminal messages to help you remember your magnificence. Your conscious mind does not need to be able to read these messages. It is your Subconscious' job to pick up the messages from each page.

If you do not resonate with any of the following messages, which are printed illegibly on several pages, either refrain from reading this book or take out a ruler and pen and cross out what does not resonate with you, while telling yourself that you are not accepting a specific affirmation. Here is a list of the subliminal messages that appear.

I AM LOVE • YOU ARE LOVE • YOU ARE A BLESSING TO THE WORLD • YOUR SOUL IS ALL-KNOWING • WE ARE ALL ONE • YOU EXCUDE HAPPINESS • YOU ARE WISE AND DISCERNING • PEOPLE AND LIFE EVERYWHERE LOVE BEING IN YOUR PRESENCE • YOU ARE LOVED • YOU ARE DIVINELY PROTECTED AND GUIDED • YOU ARE ALWAYS IN THE RIGHT PLACE AT THE RIGHT TIME • YOU ARE HEALTHY IN MIND, BODY AND SPIRIT • YOU ARE CONFIDENT • YOUR SELF ESTEEM IS HIGH • YOU ARE FOREVER EXPANDING IN YOUR KNOWLEDGE • YOU EASILY TRANSCEND PETY THINGS • YOU EASILY SEE THROUGH THE ILLUSION OF THINGS AND PEOPLE • YOU ARE A GREAT COMMUNICATOR • YOUR FRIENDS ARE FILLED WITH INTEGRITY AS ARE YOU • YOU ARE SURROUNDED BY A DIVINE SUPPORT SYSTEM • YOU LOVE YOURSELF • YOU HONOR YOUR BODY • YOUR SOUL'S EXPANSION IS OF UTMOST IMPORTANCE TO YOU • YOU ARE KIND TO LIFE EVERYWHERE • I LOVE YOU • YOUR LOVE AND ACCEPT YOURSELF COMPLETELY

The Four Gateways

Living the Inspired and Influential Life –
A Life built on Integrity and Intelligence

by

Cha~zay Sandhriel, Ph.D., C.H.

Dedication

This book is dedicated to your soul's evolution.

Special Thanks

Thank you, Cristóbal, for teaching me this most valuable lesson about the four gateways. In your graciousness and unselfishness you shared your wisdom with me. As a result my life has never been the same and it is my deepest hope that the lives of others can change and be enriched as much as mine has.

Table of Contents

Book Summary

Welcome and thank you for allowing me to accompany you on your life's journey for just a little while.

This is not a book meant to be read. This is one of those books that you "do."

This book contains an important formula that will not only simplify your life but also put your life on the fast track of true success that you can't even dream of right in this moment.

No matter your current success status, your title, your ambitions, or your current situation, if you feel like you've been paddling upstream or perhaps you've been pushing the river downhill a bit too hard, this book may just contain the solution you've been looking for.

Have you ever asked yourself one of the following questions?

"Who am I?"

"What is my life's mission?"

"Who is my life partner?"

"Should I start my own business?"

"Should I move to another country?"

"Is now the time to build a family?"

Or perhaps you've asked yourself one of the following questions?

"What's the solution to this particular problem?"

"Why do I keep doing that?"

"Why does s/he keep doing that?"

"Is s/he the one for me?

"Is now the time to start a family?"

The Four Gateways is a book about ancient Mayan wisdom that teaches us about the four doors each and every human being must walk through, no matter their life goals or current status.

Gateway 1: Fear

Gateway 2: Clarity

Gateway 3: Power

Gateway 4: Wisdom

Everyone is more than eager to walk through gateways two and four. Very few are interested in gateway four and almost all avoid gateway one like the plague.

Our assured success and completion of our life's mission, no matter what it is for each of us, can only be assured if we are willing to face all gateways and walk through them in sequence.

This book will teach you about these four gateways and how to walk through them in sequence. I will give you a formula so you can practice and get so good at, that you will be able to apply it to any and all life situations and find solutions to any problem in less than two minutes.

I'm not going to lie to you. If you're a conflict avoider and like living in the comfort zone, the exercises in this book may be challenging for some of you. Push through it anyway.

If you love to get pushed into the discomfort zone because you know that your character and soul get strengthened in the process, then you're going to love this process and breeze right through it.

The lives of most humans today prove that their lives are in shambles, discombobulated and scattered. We want things yesterday and without having to work for it.

Helen Keller once said:

"Character cannot be developed in ease and quiet. Only through experience of trial and suffering can the soul be strengthened, ambition inspired, and success achieved."

There is a way for all human beings to live a life filled with love and outstanding success. A life lived without fear, one guided by crystal clarity that leads to true inner power and eventual elder wisdom.

You're about to learn how to experience more peace, crystal clarity, true love, inner power and finally wisdom – no matter the situation you want to apply this formula to.

The individual who embarks on their life journey following these four gateways is the human being that exudes a strength and power and a charm that is irresistible and truly powerful. Success is assured.

CHAPTER 1

An Ancient Mayan Encounter

In everyone's life, at some time, our inner fire goes out. It is then burst into flame by an encounter with another human being.

Albert Schweitzer

An Ancient Mayan Encounter

Across from me sits a short, slim man who exudes a type of peace and power that my soul yearns for.

'What's his secret?' I wonder.

His name is Cristóbal. An elder from Guatemala and an original time keeper to the Mayan traditions.

Many years ago I found out that most of these elders are not reachable to mainstream society. So my wish to get an astrology reading from an elder of the Mayan traditions had been tucked away and put in a drawer until today.

Patience is indeed a virtue.

It's Sunday afternoon and we're meeting in Sedona for a two-hour reading.

Although I understand some Spanish and speak Italian, I wanted a translator present to make sure I wouldn't miss any detail.

I had been working with my Western and Eastern astrology charts for a few decades but didn't know what to expect during a reading with this amazing man, whose wisdom and knowledge had been handed down from generation to generation.

As he takes out his tools of the trade, I carefully study his demeanor. His dark skin, black hair and kind, dark brown eyes beautifully match the rest of his simple appearance.

I can tell he's in deep thought.

He asks for my birthday and then draws up a simple map, lays out stones and other items in a systematic way that only made sense to him. He looks at the chart intently, then looks at me, then looks at the chart again. And then he says to me in a calm voice:

"You are Mayan medicine woman."

"Oh no, I'm Swiss." I quickly say.

The translator chuckles and Cristóbal's eyes light up: "You are from Switzerland!?" he asks with a twinkle in his eyes.

"Yes," I respond, still wondering why he thought I was a Mayan medicine woman.

Cristóbal closes his eyes for a few seconds while the translator and I look at each other wondering what he is doing.

He then opens his eyes and looks straight at me. He puts his right hand on his heart and takes a small bow as he quietly says:

"It's an honor to meet you."

Feeling a bit uncertain of what's going on I glance over to the translator again who shrugs her shoulders. I look into those dark eyes again and reach out to touch his arm:

"No, no, the honor is all mine, Cristóbal. I've waited many years to meet you and I feel privileged to be with you here today. I'm deeply grateful."

And then he says:

"You heal as Mayan medicine woman and you do it with masculine seed energy."

'Huh?' I'm wondering to myself. 'What is he talking about? I'm not a medicine woman and what's this about a masculine seed?'

I had hoped the reading would give me more details on what to focus on over the next year or two. You know, more like the shallow things of life. I expected him to say things like: 'You will do this or that, move here or there.'

Instead Cristóbal forces me to look at gateway number one:

The gateway of fear.

Cristóbal decides to draw up my entire chart by hand and asks me to meet him the next day early in the morning.

The next morning I arrive at his guest house to find him with a hand-drawn map of my Mayan astrology chart. There were symbols and drawings and we spent the next few hours talking about my life path and the four gateways.

Over the years we have stayed in touch and his wisdom continues to enrich my life. It is with much humility I pass on my lessons to you.

Side note: Eastern and Western astrology look at the planets the *moment we are born*. Mayan astrology also takes into consideration the *moment of conception*.

The moment of conception is <u>how</u> we deliver our mission in this life. The moment of birth is <u>what</u> we deliver to this planet.

Eastern and Western astrology can give us great detail to some extent, whereas Mayan astrology goes a step further by giving us the full picture of not only what our mission is (moment of birth) but also how we can best deliver it (moment of conception).

Back to the story.

As I sit across from Cristóbal with my chart divided into quadrants, each filled with drawings, I am wondering if we will talk about something practical that would help me make some new decisions in life.

My analytical mind was hoping for grounded guidance along the lines of specifics.

By the time we were done several hours later, my entire life and the way I viewed life and people had changed.

Cristóbal senses my looking for down-to-earth advice and he sums it up like this:

"Everyone looks for clarity and power. *Clarity* is gateway number two. *Power* is gateway number three. *Wisdom* is gateway number four. Most people don't see clearly and they don't have real power because they have not yet walked through gateway number one, which is the gateway of *fear*."

He went on to explain what each of these gateways are and how to walk through them.

Life becomes a perpetual miracle zone when we walk through each of these gateways fearlessly and with courage and love.

Cristóbal explained that each of us must walk through these gateways in the right sequence for each type of clarity we are looking for, or we will never reach the last two gateways, the gateways of true *inner power* and *elder wisdom.*

This book is about these four gateways, what they are, why they are so important and how to walk through them for each set of circumstances that you may face in life.

This book is written backwards, starting with the fourth gateway - the gateway of wisdom. After understanding the four gateways we will start your work and begin with gateway one – the gateway of fear.

To make the best of this book, please have a pen and notebook handy.

CHAPTER 2

The Gateway of Wisdom

Just as treasures are uncovered from the earth, so virtue appears from good deeds, and wisdom appears from a pure and peaceful mind. To walk safely through the maze of human life, one needs the light of wisdom and the guidance of virtue.

Buddha

Gateway Four: Wisdom

This gateway has nothing to do with being book smart, having actual knowledge or your ability to regurgitate historical data. On the contrary.

Many people using intellectual common sense will miss this gateway all together because they are more interested in matters of the ego and the world of false power, rather than true wisdom.

The very rare few who make it past the gateway of fear to the gateway of clarity, who are fortunate enough to letting their fears refine their character, who are granted access to the gateway of power, will eventually end up in front of this gateway – the gateway of elder wisdom.

This is elder wisdom. And yet this gateway has nothing to do with age. Society considers many people elders because of their physical age.

At the same time so many old people are less mature than most three-year olds. Many old people become even meaner and more egotistical with age. Very few become truly wise.

Likewise, we all have heard some three year olds say things filled with such enlightened wisdom that could only come from a state of purity and utter transparency, something so many adults have lost along the way and never regained.

True elder wisdom doesn't have anything to do with age, it has everything to do with purity, living in a light of integrity and true intelligence.

It is through this gateway of wisdom where all planes and realities open up to the human mind. This plane includes the ability to see through all fears, see all outcomes and potentials with crystal clarity. Here we see people with true power and wisdom as a result of applying right thinking and making healthy choices that are always in alignment with ones highest good, including the good of life everywhere.

This doesn't mean that you have to be an elder in order to achieve this type of wisdom. It simply means that this is not a wisdom that can be achieved from reading books or attending workshops or having been married once or twice or having built a successful company.

Those things all add to enrich our lives, what really makes us reach this gateway of wisdom is the sustainability of how we respond to life and its challenges after we have obtained the true inner power that can only come from gateway three, the gateway of inner power.

You see, just because you walk through the gateway of fears once and reach the plateau of clarity, doesn't mean you have arrived at the gateway of power or the gateway of wisdom. It simply means you have overcome one tiny aspect of life. This is where the journey really begins.

It is in the field of unlimited potential (gateway two: clarity) that you are faced with a myriad of choices.

Depending on what type of choices you make, you will end up in the field of inner power or you may attempt to force that gateway open and demand that type of power because you feel entitled to it or because you're arrogant enough because of the so-called false success you have achieved in life to date.

I'm sure you can think of a few people who fall in this 'false power' category.

In order to ascend to the gateway of wisdom one must prove that they are worthy to have that type of gateway opened. And we do so by the choices we make and by how we use our personal power.

Once through the gateway of wisdom, everything seems to be available for our choosing. Whether you want information on your own life, someone else's life, your next steps in business or figure out how to help your friend in need – it's all there for the picking for you.

With this type of wisdom you can run companies that are not short lived but that last for decades, perhaps even hundreds of years.

Why? Because armed with the wisdom from this gateway comes a long-term vision about anything and everything, which will give you the insights needed to steer any project, including a company, in the direction of your choosing.

With this information, however, you do not choose selfishly, you choose selflessly. Always with others in mind and a heart and soul of servitude.

People who walk through this gateway also don't care about leaving behind legacies and they don't leave undone tasks for others to figure out at their death. They know their responsibilities while being here and they understand the impact their departure has on the world, and yet they leave behind hope and trails of goodness and fond memories for all, not trails of lawsuits and broken and bitter hearts.

Remember that there are no shortcuts to getting to the gateway of elder wisdom. This is not a quick run or sprint, this is a long and arduous journey of self-mastery, and only you can commit to your own unfolding journey.

I'm here to point the way and guide you to your own gateways, but you must turn the knob or push down the handle and walk through each door and do the actual work yourself.

CHAPTER 3

The Gateway of Power

Mastering others is strength. Mastering yourself is true power.

Lao Tzu

Gateway Three: Power

There is much to be said about the word power and clearly many in the world are hungry for it.

All wars are about power. All conflict is about who has more power over whom. Everything related to money has to do with this energy we call power. All jealousy and acts of anger have to do with power.

That's not the type of power this gateway is about.

The true power of gateway number three is about an inner power that emanates from a place of strength of character, not a place of holding a powerful position, having a gun, being famous or being an executive running a multi-billion dollar company. Those are illusory gateways of power that will never lead to gateway number four, which is elder wisdom.

Wanting worldly power is like building a house of cards. It is bound to fall.

And since life on earth is ever-so temporary and shallow, this house of false power will fall at the latest the moment you cross over into your next chapter of your journey – the moment of death.

If you're lucky, your house will fall way before and teach you an invaluable lesson about what true power is. You can then course-re-direct and start over. This time the right way.

What we leave with are the internal qualities of character we have worked towards in life. Everything external simply falls away.

Walter Russell calls these nuggets of wisdom 'gold of earth' and 'gold of heaven.' When you leave this place you can only take with you the qualities of your soul.

After you have walked through the gateway of fears and find yourself on top of the mountain tops where you have the most amazing clarity to see all angles to your situation, you find yourself stand in front of the gateway of power.

This gateway has everything to do with having power over your Self, your character and the person you want to be.

This is the place where kicking a bad habit becomes a thing of the past. Whether it's a specific behavior or an addiction to a substance or a person, you will find that you have the inner power to free yourself from anything and anyone that is not serving your highest good or the good of humanity.

This is the place where you truly know how you operate, what's important to you, what's essential to your well-being and what doesn't serve you.

This is a place where you emanate true strength from within and everyone around you sees the changes in you and they want a piece of that power.

This is a type of power that makes you walk taller, not in arrogance, but in humility. A type of power that others are attracted to, that makes others perk up and listen when you talk, because your walk is your talk and your talk is your walk.

This is also the place from where you can laugh at the future, no matter what the future holds. Whether there is plenty in your future or another drought awaits you, you know that your strength comes from a source so endless that you don't fear what's ahead. Here you are acutely in tune with yourself and others as well as life everywhere on the planet.

Not much rattles your cage here. Traffic, delays, upset employees, bosses or tragic events taking place in the world become sources of opportunities for you to respond with power and compassion.

When things don't go your way you quickly and within a few seconds define your gateway of fears and identify all levels of fears and quickly arrive at the hidden agenda fear; your own hidden agenda fear as well as those around you (explained in subsequent chapters).

And when you have stepped fully into your own magnificence through this field of power, you come to the threshold of the gateway of wisdom.

Before coming to this type of power, however, you must first walk through the field of clarity.

Sadly, the majority of the world wants false power and intellectual knowledge, which are not at all what gateways three (power) and four (wisdom) are about.

The majority of the world, especially the high-powered and influential person, wants power *over* something, whether this is a person, a company or an entire country.

And they are often more interested in book knowledge than they are in true elder wisdom that can only come from living a life that shapes and molds a character into an unshakeable prime example of what true strength of character really is.

We see this misuse of external power versus internal power often in government officials, corporate tycoons and celebrities, where fame, money and *power over others* is more important than the *servitude to others*.

We also see this type of false power being exercised against humanity by the media. The media gives the world not what it deserves to know.

Instead they feed the world whatever necessary to manipulate and entrain it just enough to keep humanity in a sedated state. While the masses are hungry for bad news and drama, which leaves them utterly powerless.

On a smaller scale we see this hunger for false power even in competitive sports. We even use terms like 'beat' or 'win' or 'conquer' to reflect which team walks away the more powerful team.

What about power between two people? Imagine two women who are jealous of each other. One is jealous of the way the other one looks, what she wears, the car she drives or the boyfriend or husband she has. Women and men can be jealous of famous celebrities they don't even know in person.

We ought to add spiritual teachers to this group too. Many of these people want others to look up to them. There are plenty of so-called spiritual teachers who are nothing more but power hungry manipulators playing on the gullibility of thirsty souls looking for guidance.

These are all states far from the gateway of true inner power. In all of these examples we have people desiring power and wanting clarity about what's important to them, but incapable of obtaining it.

This thirst for false power is everywhere around us.

People who seek this type of power are people who skip over gateways number one and two and head straight for gateway number three, the gateway of power.

These are the people that will sell their souls for fame, money and power at any cost, including the cost of might over right.

Most of these people exercise force rather than real power.

Their way of forceful living leaves behind a trail of hopelessness and poverty for others.

There is only one way to get to this gateway of power, and that's through the gateway of clarity. And the only way to get to the gateway of clarity one must first walk through the gateway of fear. There is no other way, there is no short cut, and there is no one to pay to 'let you in' through the back door there is no hidden side door either. You must do the work yourself.

CHAPTER 4

The Gateway of Clarity

Children are remarkable for their intelligence and ardor, for their curiosity, their intolerance of shams, the clarity and ruthlessness of their vision.

Aldous Huxley

Gateway Two – Clarity

Behind the gateway of clarity everything becomes clear about any and all situations. It's like looking into a crystal ball where the past and the future all meet in the 'now' to give you the complete picture of whatever situation you are faced with. It is the ultimate place where you have full use of two powerful gifts:

Magic wand number one: The ability to *think* and *reason*.

Magic wand number two: The ability to *choose* based on that thinking.

The majority of humanity likes these two magic wands but they have no clue how to use them. They don't think and would rather someone else make choices for them. Be it their parents, their spouses, their employers or their government.

For example, most humans crave being superior to animals, killing them for sport, profit and selfish gain, while at the same time they still live like animals themselves – mostly based on instinct and reactiveness.

A person living with clarity and from a place of power and wisdom lives from a place of responsiveness, which absolutely requires those two magic wands.

It is these two faculties that set humanity apart from the animal kingdom, which function purely on instinct, without the ability to reason and make constructive choices based on that thinking.

Is it any wonder then by not accepting these gifts that the world is in the state that it is in?

We live in a world where people live like sheeple, willing to be led to wherever the mighty powerful want to lead them, even if it means to the mental slaughter house where they'll be stripped of their last freedoms.

This gateway of clarity cannot be entered without first having gone through the gateway of fear.

Which is why so many people in this world are willing to live a in a state of zombie-ism, getting on a treadmill every morning to get in hideous traffic to rush to a cubicle to do a job they hate, while making someone else wealthy, to get home exhausted only to numb away the pain with cigarettes, booze, drugs, sex, mindless TV or a weekend shopping spree to make the pain go away.

This is the life of unclarity. A life that is frothed with misery and lack of clarity, only to be sedated with stress related diseases so one can die an untimely death.

When one has walked through the gateway of fear first, however, the door to the gateway of clarity appears and what's behind this gateway is the kingdom of pure potential with a 360 degree view.

Having faced and conquered your fear, this then becomes the place of empowerment. This is where you become a deliberate creator with endless opportunities and choices.

This is where you realize that instead of *reacting* to the world and people around you, you get to *respond*.

Instead of fighting one effect with another, constantly reacting to put out fires here and there, your life becomes a plethora of choices.

Each and every day turns into an exciting new buffet of unlimited choices and potential.

This is where you get to cherry pick your life's experiences based on the choices you make, which is based on you using your faculty called conscious, deliberate thinking.

It is from this place of clarity that all of your actions and experiences get to be created, course-re-directed, eliminated, chosen or dismissed. It is in this place of power and clarity that you get to create your life anyway you want to. It is a place where you take full responsibility for your actions.

And taking responsibility becomes easier and easier because you are capable of seeing the consequences of your choices *ahead of time.*

You choose based on needs, not wants. And you realize that you are happiest when your wants and needs are one and the same.

This is a place of neutrality because you see all sides clearly. It is in this place that your status increases as you make choices for yourself and others that are based on inner knowing and inner power. You do the right thing for the sake of doing the right thing, not because you're told to or because you are desperate.

Everything in life becomes smoother and more peaceful when you are clear about where you're going, what you're doing and why you're doing it and whom you want to do it with.

Whether you want more clarity in business or your personal life, choosing a life partner or which gift to buy for your friend's wedding. Having clarity saves you time and unnecessary stress.

Having clarity is like having a magic wand with a bright flashlight at the end illuminating every step of the way.

Imagine this. You are walking down the aisle towards your future spouse-to-be while thinking to yourself:

"Should I really marry this person? Is he or she really the one? How do I know that this is really going to last? Am I making a mistake? I haven't said 'until death do us part' yet, is there a way for me to back out now? Ah heck, I'm here, everyone else is here, I might as well go through with it."

Most people, I hope, would not walk down the aisle with such lack of clarity, and yet 60% of all marriages end in divorce anyways.

Where is this lack of foresight coming from?

Weren't there any red flags at the beginning that we should have or could have caught but didn't, perhaps because of some underlying fear that prevented us from seeing the dangers?

What about seeing clearly when you want to start a new business?

Many turn their life-long dream into a business reality, only to find out that it wasn't as glamorous as they hoped or thought it would be.

Through the seeming detour, however, real clarity starts to come forward through the trials and tribulations that await us along the road of discovery.

Very few people live on this earth who know at the age of two or three that they want to be this or that, and then with laser focus, and the support of their parents, turn their knowingness into a passionate career.

We can think of singers or celebrities who may have always known that they would end up on TV or on stage singing to the world.

This level of clarity is not available to most of us. For most people, life is about collecting data through opportunities that present themselves to us. We then sort through the data, saying:

"I like this. I don't like this so much."

What remains is something called expertise and hindsight, born out of the choices we have made along the way.

We then assemble these puzzle pieces and use our faculties called thinking and choosing and design a life for ourselves that suits our experience, strengths and our desire and inner drive.

To do this successfully, we need clarity or we're just stumbling around in the dark.

Seeing Into The Far Distance

When we are standing in front of the gateway of clarity without having first walked through the gateway of fear, it is like standing in front of a gateway that is not yet ready to be opened. We stand there with possibilities and also with many uncertainties.

This is where "what ifs" and "could I" and "should I" live. And later from this place we also find "I should have" and "I could have" and "If I had only" and "why didn't I" and all the other forms of Shoulditis.

Life offers enough detours, potholes and bumps in the road, without us adding to the confusion. To come to a place where the gateway of clarity is wide open, no matter the situation is to find yourself in a place of true empowerment.

All "what ifs" and "uncertainties" cease to exist when we act based on having gathered all the facts, making final decisions based on knowing. Our path is then frothed with confidence and trust in our desires and in a greater divine plan.

You may be a business executive looking to start and build a new multi-million or billion dollar company. Or perhaps you want to invest in real estate but you need clarity of what the market is going to do over the next few years or decades?

The field of clarity will provide you with a space where you can see beyond the horizon into an area where time and space seemingly cease to exist. A place of knowing, rather than a place made up of beliefs and hopeful wishing.

When the door of clarity doesn't open, it's because we have not yet faced what's behind the door of fear.

The way to this field of clarity is through the gateway of fear. The first gateway in the sequence, the most scary gateway of them all, the one we'd rather pretend doesn't exist at all, which is why so many will avoid this gateway at all cost.

Not so fast. This gateway may hold all the treasure you've been search for a long time.

Jack Canfield once said:

"Everything you want is on the other side of fear."

So instead of forcing open the gateways of wisdom, power or clarity, let's stand in front of the gateway of fear and see what's behind this gateway, shall we?

CHAPTER 5

The Gateway of Fear

"Character cannot be developed in ease and quiet. Only through experience of trial and suffering can the soul be strengthened, ambition inspired, and success achieved."

Helen Keller

Gateway One - Fear

The first gateway in the quadrant is the gateway of fear.

Just what's behind this gateway?

This is the gateway most people want to and do avoid, at any cost. Facing your fears can be frightening and uncomfortable.

If you just thought to yourself:

"What fear? I don't have any fears!"

Then you are most likely amongst those people who run straight for gateway number three: the gateway of power.

Is it power, fame or status that interests you more than anything?

Power can come in many shapes, forms, illusions and delusions.

Especially the type of power that comes from financial success, climbing the corporate ladder, reaching a certain level of fame, and so on.

If these sound familiar to you, and whether you have achieved them or are on your way to, you will most likely discover that you've been avoiding this gateway number one on countless occasions.

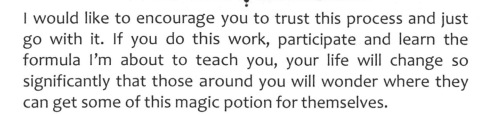

I would like to encourage you to trust this process and just go with it. If you do this work, participate and learn the formula I'm about to teach you, your life will change so significantly that those around you will wonder where they can get some of this magic potion for themselves.

Think about it, we start our lives totally unafraid and trusting. Trusting that mom and dad will catch us when we fall. In fact, we don't even have reflexes yet because falling is not a part of our experience yet. We simply trust and are blissed out most of the time.

Then we run towards that pool or walk under that majestic horse in awe, only to hear someone call out: "Be careful!"
By the time we become adults, we have learned to be afraid of many things, including strangers, and we spend the rest of our lives going from workshop to seminar and read book after book to help us undo the fears that are having such a tight hold on us.

Procrastination is another huge symptom of hidden fears lurking and begging to be resolved.

Somehow through constant repetition by the time we're so-called mature adults we have successfully convinced ourselves that the boogie man is not real after all and that there really is nothing and no one to be afraid of.

If you find yourself in this place, the fortress around your heart hasn't been challenged in a while. It's time to help break down that façade so the view over your life can become truly unrestricted.

The life lived in arrogance will never reach the gate of true power. It takes humility to get there.

Many of our fears are buried so deep beneath the surface that we're not even aware of these fears in the first place. By the time you're done with this book you will get in touch with *all* of your fears. And you will come face to face with fears you didn't even know you had.

This is truly exciting news! Because your life will never be the same as a result of the work you do throughout these pages.

Facing your fears and then transmuting them into something beneficial can be one of the most liberating and empowering experiences. So liberating in fact that it can set you on a path you never dreamed possible.

In a little bit I will share with you my all-time biggest fear and how it turned into one of my biggest passions. Before doing this work I would say things like: "I would rather die than do this."

I was serious. That's how terrified I was.

Today I can't imagine doing anything else. As a result my life has changed drastically, for the better.

I turned into a woman that I couldn't even dream of becoming – all by facing and transmuting that one fear into a brand new reality, which led me to the gateway of clarity about what my mission is in this life.

And you can do the same.

The wonderful thing about it is that once you have mastered a fear, it will never rear its ugly head at you again. In fact, your confidence will soar to such new heights that you wonder why you didn't take care of things a long time ago.

Let's do the work!

CHAPTER 6

Your Hidden Agenda
Fear

"Three things cannot be long hidden: the sun, the moon, and the truth."

Buddha

Your Hidden Agenda Fear

There is the fear and then there is the hidden agenda behind that fear.

There is the longing for a certain things and then there is the hidden agenda behind that longing.

The exercises in this book are not only to discover your fears and their hidden agendas, they are also to identify your longings and their real hidden agendas. Once you discover the hidden agenda behind why you don't do what you are passionate about, the thing you long to do ceases to have a hold on you. Instead you come up with a plan to experience your passions whenever you can.

Be honest with yourself as you go through these exercises. Only with honesty will true revelations come and help the scales fall off your eyes so you can see what's really behind the gateway of fears.

Exercise – Getting In Touch With Your Fears

Step 1: Let Your Fears Flow

Let's get started with the first exercise. Take out your notebook and a pen and write down all your fears.

No one will see this list, so let it flow out of you unrestricted. Include fears you think are silly, or too small, or too insignificant, or fears you may be ashamed of having.

They may be insignificant to someone else, but for you they may hold some sort of power. These can be justified or unjustified fears.

Some of these fears may be superficial and not cause you too much conflict in life and some of them may be debilitating.

Some may be emotional in nature and others related to finances or related to your spiritual well-being. Some may be about the past and others related to the future.

Write it all down. Just let it flow. If you need a bit of assistance in bringing those fears to the surface, I've created a cheat-sheet at the end of this book that might spur some things for you.

This exercise may take you several hours to several days. Keep this list open and ongoing.

What's going to happen over the next few days is that as soon as you give yourself permission to open this Pandora's Box, all of these fears will want to come to the surface to stick their head out to say:

> "Hi, I'm here and I'd like to be acknowledged, understood and transformed."

Over the next few days continue writing down what pops up for you.

- Don't judge the fear as valid or not that important.

- Don't fear the fear.

- Don't rate the fear.

- Don't judge *yourself* for having the fear by calling yourself names or by labeling the fear:

  "I'm such a loser."
  "This is so silly."

- Don't run away or dismiss this exercise – very important!

For now, just *acknowledge* your fears by writing them down.

Undoubtedly you will feel emotions such as uneasiness, discomfort, nervousness, sadness, anger, hopelessness, and other fears that are bringing up the situations and moments of when the fear first occurred. Some of these situations you will be able to pin point right away to when they occurred and others will be puzzling to you.

Don't analyze these emotions, just observe them for now.

Don't sulk there in these actual events of the past, just take notice of the feelings for now.

Observe yourself as you are facing these fears.

We will get back to this exercise in a little bit.

For now, continue adding to this list as things crop up and continue with the next part.

Step 2: Facing Your Fears

When I was in my mid 30s I started to feel like I wanted to leave the corporate world but I didn't know what I wanted to do. I just knew I had reached my income ceiling and I felt bored. I needed a place of unlimited potential and a place of creativity, where I could build something from the ground up.

I was looking for clarity!

I took an adult evening class that would help me get more clarity when during the break the instructor came to me, took my hands into hers and while looking intently into my eyes she said:

> "Whatever you are here to share, you need to do it by means of public speaking."

I looked at her with big eyes, raised eyebrows and my mouth dropped just a little (very unusual behavior for me, I might add). My whole body pulled back, I removed my hands from what felt like her grip and said:

> "I would rather die than speak in front of a group!"

My fear of speaking and my level of shyness and introversion were so gripping that I wouldn't even speak at a friend's bridal or baby shower. I would conveniently go to the bathroom during sharing time and wait until the sharing was over. That's how terrified I was of public speaking.

What was this woman talking about!
Me, public speaking!? She clearly doesn't know me.

And yet there was something about the intensity of the moment when she held my hands, looked into my eyes with this piercing focus and then urged me to share my work publicly. Work I hadn't even identified yet as of that evening, I might add.

This particular moment was as if time around us stood still and only the intensity of her message could be felt and heard.

I went home that night, not having gained anymore clarity about my next steps whatsoever.

Her message to me kept nudging me but I continued to brush the message off like it was a persistent, annoying little fly. I went back to work and eventually managed to silence those thoughts.

Over the next few weeks and months I grew more and more restless at work. I loved my job but something else was tugging on me and I couldn't figure out what to do.

Should I leave work and start my own company? But what would I do? How would I get business?

I was looking for clarity.

I loved real estate and always had a secret wish to build a single family home. Just for the creativeness and experience of it. Sadly, I didn't think I had what it took to undertake such a project. My confidence levels were just not there. So I tucked the secret wish away.

Someone suggested hypnotherapy to seeing how I could actually build my own home. If I could see it with my inner eye, perhaps then I would find a way of actually building my own home.

Off I went to see a hypnotherapist, who helped guide me through a visualization exercise of seeing myself build my own property.

While she was guiding me through this process I suddenly started to get visions of me speaking in front of groups. I didn't hear anything, I just saw myself standing up in front of large groups of people and giving talks.

What!? Me, speaking in front of groups of people!? Never!

And yet there it was again, this time it was in my inner vision. I decided to look at this fear once and for all and to take inventory of where this fear came from and how it had impacted my life up until this point. What I found stunned me.

Why did I have such a fear and aversion to public speaking? Where this this fear come from?

I promise to get back to this real estate vision in just a moment. First, let me take you on a slight detour.

I was an extroverted child until my first near death experience when I was five years old. Instantaneously I became a shy child, introverted and I barely spoke. My mother even used to introduce me as:

"This is the shy one. She doesn't speak much."

At school I was sitting in the last row, hoping to never be picked on by the teachers. I stuttered and I was horrible at reading out loud. My third grade teacher in particular would make fun of me and use me as an example of how *not* to read out loud.

I loved to sing but my parents would laugh at me saying that I didn't have a good voice at all and that I should focus on getting an education instead.

Everywhere I turned my wanting to express myself verbally or even via writing, I was told I wasn't good enough.

Eventually my dad would call me lazy and say that I was dumb and would never amount to anything.

My fear of public speaking was much deeper than just standing in front of a group of people and getting ridiculed.

My fear was to have to speak at all, to be heard, to have a voice, to have an opinion, and most of all, I didn't believe that what I had to share actually mattered.

Conveniently I buried this reality from my life for many decades.

Like any self-fulfilling prophecy, this one was no different. I took on jobs where I didn't have to speak, or speak much. And I certainly made sure that I never had to give speeches. I would avoid jobs where I would have to participate in management meetings and give presentations.

Unfortunately over time, the invisible ceiling above me came closer and closer and my income opportunities and professional expansion became more and more narrow.

It was decision time for me. By now I was in my mid 30s and I had managed to keep shoving this fear under the rug and avoid it at all cost.

I could choose to continue living in my comfort zone while avoiding this inability to speak up, especially in front of people. Or I could choose to face this fear and do something about it.

What I wanted more than anything was clarity.

I wasn't so much interested in losing my fear of public speaking. My life worked fine without having to speak in public, because I conveniently set it up that way. What bothered me was not knowing what to do next in life.

I knew I didn't want to spend another 30 years working for a paycheck, making someone else wealthy, when I really wanted to be free to do my own thing. But what exactly was this thing that I wanted to do?

I couldn't see clearly because this intense, gripping and debilitating fear of public speaking was so numbing, that I never even stopped long enough to see just what kind of power this fear was having over me.

Besides, why did it come up now after all these years?

Fears, much like dust bunnies under the rug, stick their head out from time to time to remind us that they're still here and still waiting to be acknowledged, understood and transformed.

When we come to a place in life where we want to make serious changes, if these changes can only be achieved by mastering one of those fears, the fear comes up like an abandoned and loyal friend to remind us that it is still there waiting patiently for some attention and resolve.

This is where we get to choose to look fear in the eye or to continue living small.

Step 3: Rate Your Fears

Take out your list again and now rate your list by placing a number in front of each of your fears. You don't have to rewrite the list if you don't want to.

I ended up typing mine up in an Excel spreadsheet so I could number my fears 1 through 15 and then sort the spreadsheet. Use whatever method works for you.

Now answer this question. Are you a "grab the bull by the horns" kind of person? The kind that prefers to have the band-aid ripped off at once or the one that wants it removed gently and very slowly?

Everyone is different, and there is no right or wrong. Choose which method works for you.

If you're anything like me, then you will get angry at the fact that you've permitted these fears to hold you back to such an extent, and you want them gone once and for all. And you'll get to a place where you're willing to do almost anything to overcome and transform yourself and those fears.

Enough is enough already. Know what I mean?

After all, this is not a dress rehearsal, this is your life.

So decide now if you want to tackle those fears with the least powerful fear first or if you want to go for fear #1 and fear #2.

I tackled my first three, most powerful and debilitating fears all together. And by doing so I noticed that my other, lesser fears automatically dissolved.

We'll continue creating an action plan around these fears, but first we have to get to the real hidden agenda fear behind the fears you've just listed.

Step 4: Discovering Your Hidden Agenda

When I finally was willing to face this fear of public speaking, I made a stunning discovery.

I have made this discovery with every fear I have faced since then and have come to the realization that most people who face their fears don't really overcome their fears until they uncover the hidden agenda behind the fear.

It is not the fears you've just written down, but the *hidden agenda* behind your fears that actually fuels your fears in the first place.

Think of it like the weed and its root. The fear is the weed itself but the hidden agenda is the root of the weed. In order to truly get rid of the fear you must pull out its root as well.

You may have faced and worked on your fears in the past and somehow the same fear keeps creeping up in one form or another. If that's the case it's because there is a *hidden agenda fear* that has yet to receive its rightful attention.

Let me explain what a *hidden agenda fear* is.

First I made a list of all the things that defined this fear of public speaking:

- Fear of failure
- Fear of looking stupid
- Fear of falling on my face
- Fear of not being able to talk at all

I call these the *first level* fears. These are the *obvious* fears, those that come to mind right away.

You've just heard my story and know that I was ridiculed when I was little, which clearly is the *anchor* of how the fear lodged into my energy field. The *anchor* of what caused the fear and the *hidden agenda fear*, however, are two completely different things.

The anchor is just the event by which the fear was brought into awareness the first time.

The *hidden agenda fear*, however, is one that you most likely are not yet aware of at all, but is the real cause of your fear in the first place.

To get to the *hidden agenda fears* we must peel back the layers by asking 'why' questions, which eventually lead to what I call the *second level* fears.

As I started to dig deeper about my fear of public speaking, I discovered that beyond fear of failing, looking silly, and so on, I was really worried about the following:

- Fear that public speaking would turn me into a person I didn't know or recognize.

- Who am I really when I'm at my best?

- What happens if I'm actually successful at this public speaking thing?

- Who would I be then?

- What sort of responsibilities would face me then?

- What if I'm actually great at this and make a lot of money, what would I do with so much money?

It wasn't the fear of failing that frightened me, it was the fear of *success* and the *unknown* of who I would become that terrified me more than anything.

1. My *first level fear* was fear of *failing.*
2. My *second level fear* was fear of *success.*

Digging deeper into what I call *third level fears,* I continued to pull back the layers even more, the real fear of not knowing who I would turn into if I was actually going to like public speaking was the fact that my comfortable little life would change.

- What if I changed so much that my husband didn't like me anymore?

- Or what if I didn't like him anymore?

- What if I was asked to travel to speak and it would take me away from our little baby?

The thought of losing what was known to me (my current life style and my family) along with my freedom was nauseating to me.

The unknowingness of "what if" caused me more fear than any of the more evident fears on the surface, such as fear of saying something silly.

1. My *first level fear* was fear of *failing.*

2. My *second level fear* was fear of *success*.

3. My *third level fear* was *fear of losing my freedom*.

I kept asking 'so what' questions and found *fourth level fears.*

- The fear of having to bare my heart on my sleeve in front of strangers.

- To be vulnerable and to humble myself in front of an audience.

- To be honest and share things about my life that I really wanted to keep buried.

The shy hermit in me wanted nothing to do with exposure.

I would have to talk about the skeletons in my closet! What then?

The judgement and misunderstandings that would come from strangers.

- Is it really worth it?

- Why would I want to be that raw and naked on a soul level?

- Would I even like myself if I dug up all the dark sides of myself and shared them with an audience?

I had found my *hidden agenda fear*!

Beyond fear of *failure*, fear of *success*, fear of losing my *freedom*, there laid the fear of being fully *exposed* and *naked* on a *soul* level, losing my *privacy*, having to talk my walk meant to walk my talk. Having to be responsible. Being a role model.

Plato says it like this:

> "We can easily forgive a child who is afraid of the dark; the real tragedy of life is when men are afraid of the light."

I was not afraid of the light itself but of the light others would see me in.

Now I had my work cut out for me. I knew the real culprit of my avoiding being a public speaker. Now I was in a place of empowerment. I could now reason through all those anchors and experiences, go back and revisit some of these issues, take classes and work on myself.

My fear of being exposed had to do with my first near death experience at the age of five. When I came back I tried to explain to my mother that this life was just a dream and that the other side was real. She dismissed it as non-sense and said to never talk about it again.

Clearly my fear tried to peak its head out when I went to school but I allowed myself to be squashed by my teachers and parents. Eventually I gave up and much of my life was lived with this fear being my guide. I took jobs that didn't allow me to use my speaking abilities and I married a husband who didn't ask me any questions. How convenient!

Today, by the way, I'm frequently asked to speak about my near death experiences and yes, I wrote a book about it called *I'm Dying, Shit! Not Again!*

Once I was equipped with knowing what my real hidden agenda fear was, I could take hypnotherapy sessions that went far beyond just the fear of public speaking.

I now could actively rewire the stories I had been telling myself all these years.

I had the power to change my introverted and shy nature to be whatever I wanted it to be.

When I found the answers to these *hidden agenda fears* is when the 'Aha' moments came, which gave me everything I needed to come up with a game plan to work with these fears.

Public speakers often have inflated egos and are quite arrogant. They're more into techniques, looking good on stage and achieving power and fame, along with earning lots of money.

These are often people who have bypassed the gateway of fear and headed straight for the gateway of power. Sadly, these people emit the false type of power that is shallow and based on vanity and superficiality and often sprinkled with an extra serving of arrogance.

They are public speakers because they want to be acknowledged, have their name written on a plaque somewhere and because it gives them fame.

These people miss the point all together.

To seek out public speaking as a career comes from a place of ego, vanity and arrogance.

To become a public speaker by accident or based on need or an invitation because you have something of value to share and are invited to share with a group comes from a place of inner power and value. You're called to bring hope and inspiration to an audience, not to flash your know-how.

This speaker comes from a place of humility and gratitude. They don't have a personal agenda other than hopefully making a difference in just one person's life.

This person understands that it's never about them; it's always about the audience that is starving for nuggets of wisdom.

When I finally realized that no one is there *for* me or *because* of me but everyone is there for themselves, is when all my fears ceased to exist.

When this realization finally clicked in, I was able to instantly stop worrying about form or technique.

All the external hoopla we worry about, which is always ego related anyways, fell away and it became about being real and wholesome, to speak from moment to moment, always authentic and real, and preferably without any notes.

I will get back to this story in a little bit. It's now time for you to peel back the layers of your own fears.

Remember what's most important when facing your fears is to discover your first-, second-, third- and fourth-level fears. You may have only three levels, and you may discover that you have five or six levels.

Ask "why" and "so what" questions and keep digging until you come to the real culprit of your fear.

I have learned that the first few reasons why we are afraid of something, anything, is usually just the shallow surface stuff. The real fear is buried within the *hidden agenda*. Allow that *hidden agenda* to be uncovered because that's where you gem stone can be found.

Step 5: Finding Your Own Hidden Agenda Fears

Take out your workbook again. Now it's time for you to peel back the layers on those fears and discover your own hidden agenda behind each of those fears.

Remember that not everything that meets the eye is what it seems. Your *real fear* is the *root* of your fear, not what you actually think it is.

Here are just a few examples of fears and their possible hidden agendas:

Dating

- Level 1: Fear of dating
- Level 2: Fear of intimacy
- Level 3: Fear of being cheated on and lied to
- Level 4: Fear of not being enough and not needing anyone. If I don't need anyone, I will most likely end up alone. Ending up alone I may end up a bitter old man or woman and live out my life in a nursing home without children to visit me.

The real *hidden agenda fear* here is about *loneliness* and being *abandoned*, not fear of dating or fear of intimacy or even being cheated on.

Paradoxically, the fear itself will most likely assure the self-fulfilling prophecy. In other words, the person will choose to remain single because the fear of being left or abandoned is bigger than the fear of actually dating.

Your fear levels may look very different for each of these categories.

Your fear may trace back to your own child hood and you may be afraid that your date will eventually become your spouse and over time become just like your mom or dad, an alcoholic or drug addict, and you really don't want to go through that again.

Remember that anchors are not usually tied to the fear but they are what bring the fear to your awareness the first time.

Starting peeling back the layers!

Starting Your Own Company

- Level 1: Fear of starting my own company
- Level 2: Fear of leaving a safe and secure job
- Level 3: Fear of business failure (running out of money, not having enough clients)
- Level 4: Fear of not being about my highest calling

In this example the real fear is not failure of the new business venture but failure to not bring out ones true life mission.

If you are absolutely certain that you are about your highest calling, the fears of competition and running out of money cease to exist.

Common sense still needs to prevail but the overall fear of failure won't even be a part of your experience – provided you are truly about what makes your heart go pitter-patter.

Please note that any of these examples could have completely different items for levels two, three or four. You may not even need four lines to peel back the layers. Or you may need more levels.

It is not very likely that unless you are familiar with this process, that you know what your *hidden agenda fear* is right from the get-go. Even if you think you know what your *hidden agenda* is, there is most likely still something else that is awaiting your discovery.

Trust the process and do the work!

Right now this seems like a lot of work but believe me when I say that when you get the hang of this, you will get to your *hidden agenda fears* in less than a minute or two.

You will also get great at asking other people just the right questions that will let you see *their hidden agenda* fear right away.

How will this benefit you and them? Being able to help others will put you in a place of service and one of utter understanding and compassion. From this place you will stand before your own gateway of clarity as well as theirs. You can then help them cross the threshold and turn their own fears into treasures.

Please note that from here you will also reach the gateway of power. Here you have a choice to abuse this power with this knowledge of their fears. And if you abuse this power for your own selfish gains or to hurt others in any way, your house of cards will crumble. Instead, choose to respect this place of true, inner power and help others reach that same level.

How you will know when you have reached all levels of fears and their underlying fears?

You will know when you reach the gateway of clarity.

For as long as you are asking questions of clarity you have not yet discovered the *hidden agenda fear*. Keep digging.

Here is another example.

Fear of Sales

A client of mine was turned off all her life by sales people. She had an experience involving her mother and a salesman that came to their door when she was just a little girl, which left a permanent, sour taste in her mouth, and she disliked anything having to do with sales from that moment on.

As this little girl grew up and climbed the corporate ladder she was always very aware of this turn-off in her life and she did her best to structure her life to avoid sales at all cost.

Over time, however, she too realized that her career was hindered by this lack of experience and she wanted to work on this uncomfortable fact in her life.

First she read books, went to workshops and learned how to write her own sales copy on her website. She became quite good at it compared to where she had come from.

And yet when she became her own boss she realized that the fear of having to sell her services to get clients was so debilitating, that she chose to give up her business instead of pushing through her fears and discomforts.

She knew exactly where her fear had come from. She even went to therapy to overcome her fear. Nothing helped.

She gave up her business and went back to work as an employee but unhappy about having been defeated by her intense fear.

Years later she took another chance on herself and vowed to herself to do whatever it took to master this fear.

Together we worked on her list of fears and as we started to peel back the layers to discover her fear's *hidden agenda* we discovered that she wasn't afraid of sales at all, she was deathly afraid of having to approach men!

She had no problem telling women about her services but she refused talking to men about her business.

She associated approaching men with aggressiveness, which is so contrary to how she was raised by her traditional parents.

It had been instilled on her to never, ever approach a man as a woman but to signal to him that she was approachable in an effort to letting him make the first move. Of course the advice she received had nothing to do with business and everything to do with her romantic life. But the impact this teaching made on her in combination with the salesman who showed up at her door when she was a little girl was engraved so deeply in her that she completely missed her real *hidden agenda* fear all together.

What did she do?

She made a switch in thinking and saw herself as half of the whole, offering an invaluable service to her male clients whom would otherwise not reach the same results if they were to work with a man.

In other words, she saw herself as an asset to these men, instead of an aggressive intruder making the first move into a business relationship with a male client. She was able to see clearly for the first time and when she did, she became a high income earner with most of her clientele being male.

Do you see how her original fear of being a sales person to finding her fear's *hidden agenda* is almost like looking at two different Universes?

At first glance they don't seem related at all and it's only after she went through these exercises that this real fear of hers got a chance to say:

> "Hi, I'm here, I'm a real fear and I would like to be acknowledged and transformed into something so I can serve you instead of frighten you."

Fear then, becomes your greatest ally. If you let it!

Don't dismiss these exercises. Let you fears come talk to you.

Face them, acknowledge them, understand them and work with them to find the real culprit. When you do, you will have created a platform from which you can now come up with a feasible, easy to follow step-by-step plan on turning your fears into your biggest blessings.

CHAPTER 7

Creating Your Action Plan

"Thinking will not overcome fear but action will."

W. Clement Stone

Transmuting Your Fears

I love the word transmutation. It means to turn one thing from one energy or substance into another. Water into steam or mist. A caterpillar into a butterfly. A fear into a joy. A failure into success.

As with everything you undertake in life, once you have faced your fear (step 1) and you have uncovered the *hidden agenda* of your fear (step 2), it is now decision time. Time to face the music, as the saying goes.

Now that you know your hidden agenda fears, what are you going to do with this knowledge?

You can run. Yes, you can. And you can continue living the way you do now, or you can let your higher Self take you to unknown heights, which hold rewards far beyond your wildest dreams.

Here is what I did. I made a list of all my fears. There were 15 of them. Then I rated them by intensity. Fear one was public speaking, fear two was the fear of flying.

I then made a choice to tackle the most intense two fears first. You may decide to tackle the least intense fears first. I have found, however, that taking on the biggest fears will automatically dissolve all or most of the other fears as well, as if by magic.

Why is this?

Because transforming one of your fears that previously was debilitating and numbing, will cause your level of power, courage and empowerment to create a new type of energy of confidence within you and around you that will make you wonder why you ever waited so long to overcome these fears.

Most importantly, once you have walked through the gateway of fear and entered through the gateway of clarity, you will automatically come upon the gateway of inner power. From there you will enter the gateway of wisdom. With the lessons you learn from each of these gateways you will be equipped to deal with the remaining fears on your list in a completely different way.

Remember Helen Keller's words:

> "Character cannot be developed in ease and quiet. Only through experience of trial and suffering can the soul be strengthened, ambition inspired, and success achieved."

This is what you are doing when you do this work. You are strengthening your character through which new ambitions will be inspired and your success will be ensured.

Just make sure you make the right choices when you get to gateway number three – the door of power. This gateway is a trap for many and will bring out your best and also your worst.

Always choose wisdom over might. Choose humility over arrogance.

Create an Action Plan

Once I identified my fears I then set a deadline for myself and came up with a plan to strategically work on transforming and mastering these fears.

I gave myself *two years* to transform my fear of public speaking and the fear of flying. I got it done in half the time.

Here is how I did it:

I took every opportunity at work to give presentations. When I needed to give training to co-workers, I would break the presentations down into small groups of 5-6 employees so I could give the same presentation ten times.

To me this was practice and exposure, each giving me the opportunity to feel more comfortable and to do better next time.

I signed up for public speaking practice meetings. I cancelled many times because I was so afraid, only to go back the next week.

I discovered that I was more comfortable giving small presentations at work than talking in front of strangers. I would get sick to my stomach, lose my voice, get weak knees, stutter, get shaky hands and shake all over. It was horrible. But I pushed through. I kept going. Then I would cancel again. And I kept going back, until I finally stopped cancelling because I eventually realized that cancelling was just ridiculous and childish.

At the same time I agreed to enroll myself in one adult learning class per month and agreed to raise my hand at every opportunity when asked a question by the instructor. These are things I would never do before, but I wanted to push myself into a discomfort zone.

When a friend had a baby- or bridal shower, instead of running to the bathroom to hide out, I would push myself into the discomfort zone and raise my hand and ask if I could share first.

I also enrolled in a one-year mentorship program that would ask us to meet 8 times throughout the year in different parts of the country.

I was forced to not only speak and give presentations to this mentorship group of 30 people, I was also asked to fly to these locations.

Fear of flying was my second biggest fear at that time. It was a strange fear given that I wanted to be a flight attendant when I was a teenager. I've lived in half a dozen countries and had flown to many countries before. The anchor for this fear was born with the birth of my daughter.

I wasn't afraid of flying, my *hidden agenda fear* was that my daughter would grow up without her mother.

The fear of flying was easier to overcome because it was an internal fear that didn't require me to stand in front of a group of people.

My action plan considered of me taking several trips by airplane and taking out some life insurance on myself, just in case, to assure that my husband would be able to pay off the mortgage on our home so that our daughter could grow up in the home she was used to.

Once I made sure that my family would be okay if something happened to me, the fear subsided.

> "Thinking will not overcome fear but action will."
> **W. Clement Stone**

My action plan took me to first take a trip one hour away, then two hours away, then four, then six. Then I flew to Europe.

Overcoming the fear of flying was a piece of cake compared to the fear of public speaking.

You will find that some of your fears take longer than others. Keep at it. Don't give up.

Remember my story about wanting to build my own home?

During this mentorship program and by slowly transmuting fears into victories, I mustered up enough courage to go out and buy my own new construction home. The home wasn't finished yet, it was out of State and it would become my first rental property.

I didn't want the hypnotherapy go to waste and what I saw with my inner vision was strengthened by the inner work that took place as I pushed through the fear of public speaking.

After a year of doing my work I had bought more single family homes, each time while they were still in pre-construction. By the time tenants moved in, I already had positive cash flow on my properties. I was so stoked about my success and my new found passion, that I reduced my working days to four days a week, then three days, while I was traveling the U.S. looking for new properties to buy.

I went back to my hypnotist to get another shot of inner vision so I would find the courage to actually buy a raw piece of land, on which I would build my own property.

Within a week I was back on the airplane to look for land instead of looking for properties to buy. I met with a few developers, bought some land, and started to build my own single family homes.

I had so much fun and found my new job so exhilarating, that I just needed to let others know about how easy it was to buy out-of-State properties.

I contacted the Learning Annex, who at that time still held adult learning workshops around the U.S., and asked if they would allow me to teach a class. They booked me for two sessions right away.

All was well, except now push came to shove.

Sharing amongst fellow employees, being a workshop participant or sharing in front of friends at bridal showers had become easy.

This was a whole other ball game - me as the facilitator. Teaching an actual workshop to strangers, something I had never done before.

I had 68 people registered for my first class, 98% of whom were men. I had never taught in front of group of men and all the work and training I had done the previous year went out the window.

I felt new fears creeping in and I had four weeks to master them. I felt thoroughly overwhelmed.

Instead of facing my fear, I ran away. I called the Learning Annex and lied to get out of my commitment.

I felt terrible! Not only about lying to them, mostly about lying to myself and letting down 68 people.

Remorse set in almost immediately after canceling the class. The day after and I called them back to apologize and tell them that I would teach the class after all. They had already issued refunds to all 68 people and were not able or willing to call them all back.

I had blown a tremendous opportunity. This was a huge learning curve for me.

Mercifully, they kept my second date in tact under the condition that if I cancelled on them again, that I would not be accepted as a Learning Annex instructor. With this type of pressure, do you think I did whatever it took to keep my commitment? You betchya!

When the time came I totally rocked the workshop. It was my first workshop with this many people and given that public speaking would get me nauseated, dizzy, shaky and put me seriously in a place where I wanted to run up the banana tree, I was ecstatic to discover how much I actually loved facilitating.

I remained a Learning Annex instructor for many years, spoke to several real estate groups and ended up speaking on stage with Robert Kiyosaki, who is the author of Rich Dad Poor Dad, in front of thousands of people.

Who would have thought?

One Thing Leads To Another

I am sharing this story with you to show how one thing can lead to another. What now may be your greatest fear can easily turn into a great blessing. Give it a chance!

Over the years my speaking unfolded from giving left-brained, factual real estate data to a mainly male audience to teaching business planning courses to low income women.
I don't teach real estate workshops anymore. My work has evolved to mentoring and facilitating transformational work.

Today I work with executives, CEOs, presidents, government officials and celebrities on a one-on-one basis teaching them my inter-connectedness protocol.

These are high-powered, highly visible influencers who are looking to transform their lives and consequently their businesses and how they show up in the world.

If it wasn't for my having faced and then mastered my all-time biggest fears, I would never in a million years have the courage and the know-how that it takes to be a transformational mentor to such high-powered and influential people.

You too may find that you get to know yourself in a way that you can't fathom now.

When you start to work with your list of fears and you pro-actively expose yourself to transcending your fears by pushing yourself into the discomfort zone, you will come across some amazingly pleasant new information about yourself that you didn't know before.

And over time you will carve out your own niche and market by simply being you.

When you show up authentic, letting your light shine to a hungry world whose souls are thirsting for your soul's sparkle, the world becomes your oyster and you can do what you want, work with whom you want and charge premium rates without flinching.

Create Your Action Plan

Let's do a quick summary of what you've done so far.

- By now you have created your list of fears.

- You have categorized them into levels of intensity.

- You have made a decision of which fear(s) you want to tackle first. Do you want to begin with your most intense fear first? Or do you want to take the slow road?

- You then have completed the exercise to finding your fears' hidden agenda.

This is by far the most important step. If you have not yet found your fears' hidden agenda, do not proceed. Instead, go back to peeling back the layers.

Sometimes finding your fears' hidden agenda comes to you in a dream, while you're driving, or perhaps someone tells you something about yourself that is hinting at what your fear's real hidden agenda could be.

Pay attention. All information is valid. You'll know when it hits you.

Assuming you have your fear's hidden agenda, the real fear so to speak, it's time to come up with a game plan to transmute and transform this energy.

All fears want to be acknowledged, understood and given the opportunity to be used beneficially (to transform) rather than to be avoided. The steps above have now led you to the transformation stage.

You're now in the ring with the wild stallion and it's your job to train the wild horse without breaking its spirit. This takes patience, most of all with yourself, and it takes commitment – to you and the stallion (the fear) and a whole lot of forgiveness for when you fall off the wagon.

A good way of seeing a different outcome for your fear is to see the opposite of your fear.

Instead of me feeling and seeing myself fall on stage, stumble over my own words and stutter and make a fool of myself, I saw the opposite:

- I saw myself speak with eloquence and grace, with confidence and knowledge of my subject.

- I was authentic and real and in the moment.

- I was not there for myself, I was there to serve the audience.

I saw myself like this in my inner vision over and over until I became that.

There is a saying that says: "Fake it till you make it."

I disagree. I'd like you to adopt this one instead: "Visualize it till you become it."

You must become that which you wish to be. And never, ever imitate someone else. You will only be imitating someone else, who may also be imitating someone else. All the while the real magnificence of you in actuality is much better. Never focus on anyone else. Always focus on becoming a better version of yourself.

Rumi said it best:

> "Everyone is seeking the world for treasure when the real treasure is you."

You will have to take your fear's opposite and visualize yourself in that opposite again and again until it becomes a part of you.

If you can't do this by yourself, seek out a hypnotist to help you with guided visualization.

Getting guided visualization sessions became so important for me that I became a certified hypnotist myself. Working with my highly influential people I had no choice but to pass on this amazing gift to them. And the results are nothing short of miraculous.

All treasure can be found in the mind! Start with the sanctity of your own mind by feeding it the positive results that you want to see.

The trick is in finding a good hypnotist that will not feed you *their* visions but someone that is capable of guiding you to *your* own visions. In order to do that, you need to be able to tell him or her of the visions that you would like them to instill in you. And you can only do that by coming up with the opposite of your fears.

Let's look at some examples of finding the opposite of various fears.

Fear of Loneliness, Being Cheated On or Lied To

For you, you may have a fear of failing relationships, of being cheated on or lied to, or of ending up alone. Instead of hanging out in that miserable place, write down its opposite.

Take out another piece of paper and draw a line down the middle. On the left side write down your hidden agenda fear and on the right side write down its opposite – whatever its opposite is.

Don't write down what you want, I simply want you to write down its opposite.

In this example, if you're fear has to do with loneliness or being lied to or cheated on, I want you to envision yourself in your home with your partner, see yourselves communicate effectively and lovingly.

See yourselves be honest with each other every day.

Perhaps you come up with a ritual of spending the first 20-30 minutes sitting at the kitchen table talking about each of your day, reconnecting with each other after having been apart all day. See yourself go to bed at the same time, cuddling up. See yourself waking up with each other, cuddling before getting up.

See the closeness between you two. See yourself trust each other.

Once you have discovered your hidden agenda fear and then identified its opposite, it's time to come up with a plan on achieving this type of intimacy and closeness with someone.

Note: You can do this guided visualization of seeing opposites for all your fears. Your first level, second level, third level and your hidden agenda fears.

Once you see the opposite, ideal picture of what you really can achieve, ask yourself what steps you can take to achieve such results.

In this sample case, if you're single, then whom are you going to practice with? The answer is:

Everyone!
Most people are waiting for that special someone with those specific qualities to show up. They somehow believe that this reality can't exist until that person has entered their life.

That's not true at all. On the contrary.

You see, if you already had this type of closeness with those who are in your life, then you wouldn't be missing a partner. The fact that you have this type of fear (loneliness) should be a signal to you that your current relationships are lacking closeness.

So while you're single, create this type of life right now with everyone who is already in your life. Even the people you can't imagine this type of closeness with.

Practice with your other family members, your children, your siblings, your neighbors, your other friends, your co-workers, even your boss.

This will take some commitment on your part.

If you are a shy person like I am, and initiating conversation doesn't come easy to you, you may have to come up with a daily challenge for yourself.

For example:

- Initiate one conversation with a co-worker or neighbor per day.

- Initiate one conversation with a total stranger per day.
- Give one genuine compliment to one woman and one man every day.

Come up with your own *discomfort zone* and remember to be gentle with yourself. You don't have to do all of these if just one of these is making you want to run for the banana tree. Make it challenging but not so challenging that you end the day feeling like a failure if you couldn't do it.

The next step is to become that which you so dearly want.

Are you afraid of being cheated on, left or abandoned, ending up alone?

Instead of waiting for that to happen just so you can say "I knew it, it was only a matter of time," I want you to start practicing by being the person that doesn't abandon others, that doesn't cheat on others, doesn't lie to others.

Become that person first to others without worrying about when the person will show up who will share their life with you.

Most of all, you would want to practice not abandoning yourself, not lying to yourself or others. This includes not abandoning these exercising and mastering your fears. Remember, it's all about you. It always has been about you, and it will always be about you and only you.

And when you truly understand this on a soul level, you understand that by being the real, authentic you, you also give others permission to be their own real, authentic selves.

You then can be the best friend they've ever had, the best husband, the best wife, the best boss, the best employee, and so on.

Be a good partner to yourself and others first, before you attract and live the real thing with your desired life partner so that when she or he shows up, you've not only had plenty of practice, but you now expect no less but the truth and nothing but the truth.

Fear of Business Failure

What if your fear is leaving your job and starting your own business?

Remember to find the real fear first by uncovering its hidden agenda. In our above example, the real fear is to be about your highest calling. This fear in particular is there for most people I meet, for the simple fact that most people are not about their highest calling. They know this on some level and it expresses itself in ways of anger, irritation, addiction, unhappiness, depression, infidelity, and more.

It also expresses itself in people asking questions such as "who am I" or "where did I come from." These are all questions of a person seeking clarity (gateway two). And seeking clarity comes as a result of there being an underlying fear (gateway one).

In this above example, the real fear is being about your true purpose.
What if you don't know what your real mission here is?

You are employed, you like your job or maybe you hate your job. There is a calling from within to leave your job and start your own business.

You have a business in mind but clearly, the fact that you are scared is a red warning sign that perhaps you're close but not quite there yet. When you know your soul's highest calling all doubt is burned away and you move forward without fear.

Take out a new piece of paper. Date it.

Write down what your life would look like if you were indeed about your highest calling and money was no issue. Here are some questions for you to answer about your ideal work. Let your imagination flow:

- What do you do all day? Describe your perfect work day.

- Who do you work with? Describe your ideal clients in detail.

- What do your clients say about you and your products or services? Write up some testimonials you'd like to see. Make them up and keep them in a safe place so you can compare notes later.

- What do your clients experience as a result of using you products or services? Write down specific changes your clients experience.

- How has your overall life changed as a result of you living your highest calling?

- Where do you live? Who lives with you? Where do you vacation? What car do you drive? What does your house look like? What do you do for fun? What kind of friends are you surrounded by? What makes life worth living?

Don't dismiss this exercise. This is not wishful thinking. This is you in creation mode.

After you've answered these questions, answer this question:

- What will the rest of my life look like if I choose <u>not</u> to overcome this fear and I remain in my current position?

Now imagine yourself having come to the end of your life. It's now years later and you find this piece of paper again. How do you feel knowing that you never moved forward with your dream because you let your fear keep the upper hand?

Are you regretful? Do you wish you had another run at life? Are you feeling defeated and disappointed in yourself that you let fear hold you back so many years ago?

The good news is that you are not there yet, or you probably wouldn't be reading this book. And if you're a breathing human being there is still time to get things done.

I'm hoping this gives you enough courage to say:

> "I will not let these fears control me. I will master them and become the best version of myself that I've come to be."

When I finally shifted my mind around the fear of public speaking, it was because I realized that my speaking to groups was not about me at all. It was all about my audience. I was just a vessel, a vehicle delivering information, being utilized to share something with a hungry audience that needed and wanted something that I had.

My fear turned from fear to compassion.

In one instant, instead of fearing all these eyeballs staring at me, I came to love them and realized my mission was to give them the nourishment they had made an effort to come here and receive. They weren't there for me. They were there for themselves.

Who was I to withhold that information?

When I finally realized that it wasn't about me, that it's never about me, I could come from a place of utter service and the thousand pound boulder on my shoulders lifted. What freedom.

The real miracle comes when you realize that you are being given everything you need the moment you are serving others, without selfish agenda whatsoever.

The same applies to your fears about relationships or fears about starting a business. The same applies to fears about money.

You are not of service to people on this planet if you are lacking the financial means to performing your job, whatever that job is. Money is just one of the tools that allow you to spread your work to a hungry audience who is desperate to hearing what you have to share.

Don't withhold your precious self from those who are here to learn and grow because of something you have to share.

Share yourself, freely, generously and honestly.

CHAPTER 8

Fear of Money

"Wealth is the ability to fully experience life."

Henry David Thoreau

Fear of Financial Shortcomings

Money has such an intense hold on most people that it deserved its own chapter.

Money fears are huge, for almost anyone that I know of.

The fear of financial shortcomings or failures is directly tied to our physical well-being. I grew up with a mother who grew up at the German border during the war and scarcity has been her steady companion throughout life. Even to this day.

In fact, the Readers Digest in Canada did a survey around the world, asking 16 countries and 150 respondents from each country, to rate amongst four of the top rated fears:

- Fear of losing your looks
- Fear of going broke
- Fear of public speaking
- Fear of being alone

The U.S. top rated fear for men was the fear of going broke. A whopping 52% of men (and 32% of women) rated this as their top fear.

Other 'advanced' countries were no better when it came to this fear of going broke:

Country	Men	Women
U.S.	52%	32%
Canada	47%	33%
England	49%	38%
S. Africa	50%	41%
Australia	40%	25%

Source: http://readersdigest.ca

In Western Society this fear of going broke tops the other fears, including the one of being alone. Although in other countries such as Mexico, Brazil, China, Philippines, India, Russia and others, the fear of being alone triumphs over the fear of going broke.

Our mother instilled this energy of scarcity in my sister and myself and for the longest time the fear of money, not having it or having too much of it and having to be responsible for it, consumed my life. My ambivalence and misunderstanding of money caused me to sit on a money-merry-go-round.

Consequently, my life reflected my fear around money. I became a multi-millionaire and then I lost it all and became homeless, sleeping in my car for seven months.

Today I live in a place of neutrality and detachment when it comes to the energy of money.

I somehow had to grow up with this energy of attachment to money and learn what it was like to have plenty of it and then go to the other extreme and learn what it was like not to have enough pennies to buy myself a hot cup of tea in the cold of winter.

These were *my* lessons. I don't wish my journey on anyone while at the same time I wouldn't trade it for anything.

Today, the fear of money, having too much of it or not enough of it, has completely left my presence.

I had to experience both spectrums of the story so I would arrive at a place where I see money for what it really is: a means of exchange to keep the work I do circulating and to obtain the things needed to spread my work.

Many of you reading this, however, are not yet in this boat and you do fear money or people who have it. Or perhaps you have lots of money but judge those who don't have it and live on social services.

Perhaps you're fine right now but you're fear is projected into the future and you're afraid that someone will come swindle you out of your hard-earned money or perhaps you're afraid you're getting over-quoted every time you want to hire a contractor, just because you live in a nice house or drive a nice car.

Or maybe you're afraid that the world is going completely bonkers because of its greed and lust for money and you're in a state where you wish money didn't exist at all.

Whatever your surface fear is, remember that there is also the *hidden agenda* behind your first level fear. And when it comes to money I can guarantee you that there is always a *hidden agenda fear* behind it. This hidden agenda fear, however, is different for everyone and only you can dig deep to find out what your hidden agenda is.

I can share a few of mine and share a few of some of my friends' to help you with this.

Money Fear Example 1:

- First level fear: not having enough money

- Second level fear: not being able to buy food or pay for shelter or utilities

- Third level fear: not being able to keep your children warm, fed and safe

- Hidden agenda fear: failing as a spouse or parent

Money Fear Example 2:

- First level fear: not earning enough money

- Second level fear: not getting paid what you're worth

- Third level fear: not finding a mate that is on your level

- Hidden agenda fear: not feeling worthy to be loved unless you earn a specific amount

Money Fear Example 3:

- First level fear: having my home or retirement taken from me (divorce, swindlers, bad business choice, etc.)

- Second level fear: working hard all life only to lose it and end up with nothing

- Third level fear: becoming homeless or having to rely on others or social services (false sense of pride)

- Hidden agenda fear: becoming a burden to others

Money Fear Example 4:

- First level fear: not earning as much as my colleagues are earning even though you are doing the same job or are more qualified

- Second level fear: shame and embarrassment

- Third level fear: being stuck on the treadmill without any hope of getting ahead

- Hidden agenda fear: never truly experiencing or living out what your soul truly wants to express; sense of stuckness and lack of freedom

---

If it wasn't for me having experienced both, plenty and lack and everything in between, I would probably still fret about money.

When I look back on how much time I wasted worrying about not having enough or being taken advantage of or fretting about my investments or my future, I realize how much precious energy I wasted worrying about something that wasn't even a reality.

When I realized that time is the most precious commodity any of us have, no matter our status, name or perceived importance in life, I realized that everyone's time is equally as precious.

Once we give our time, we give something that we will never get back. Time then is our most prized possession.

In reality it's not even something we possess. It's more like time cradles us in its own arms back and forth like the swing of a pendulum.

Tic. Tac. Tic. Tac.

What you do with your daily, allotted time allowance of 24 hours is completely up to you. You can work it away. You can sleep it away. You can learn it away. You can drink it away. You can eat it away.

What are you doing with your daily allotted 24 hours of the day?

Back to money. So how do you deal with this fear of money exactly?

Worrying about money is to escape into the past or chase the future while completely missing the current moment.

In this current moment in which you are reading these lines, you have no need for money at all. You are fine just as you are, right now, wherever you are.

And in this moment, a few seconds later, you are still fine exactly as you are.

Exercise: What Do You Love?

Take out your notebook again and leave some space to the right where you will be creating four columns marking each line with a checkmark.

It will look something like this example:

Things I Love To Do	I Do This Now	I Don't Do This Now	Costs Money
1. Working Out	✓		✓
2. Take elaborate trips around the world		✓	✓✓✓✓
3. Going to the movies	✓		✓
4. Spending time it with friends and family	✓		⋮
5. Hiking	✓		⋮
6. Great conversation	✓		⋮
7. Going to workshops	✓		✓✓
8. Reading	✓		⋮
9. Cooking	✓		✓

Instructions:

Column 1: In the left column write down all the things you love to do.

Column 2: Place a checkmark next to each of the items that you are currently doing.

Column 3: Place a checkmark next to the items that you would like to do but don't currently get to do.

In our example here this person would love to take elaborate trips around the world but they are not currently getting to do that.

Column 4: Place a checkmark in this column if this costs something; put two checkmarks if it costs more than just a little and put three or four checkmarks if it is really expensive.

If the activity doesn't cost you any money, such as reading a book, put a line there or keep it blank.

Here is a little help if you're unsure of how many checkmarks your activity costs:

Any time you spend a large chunk of money, you may want to use four checkmarks. Things like owning your own home, or buying investment properties, getting a new car, or traveling around the world. These may justify getting four checkmarks.

Attending workshops or getting a new diploma or certification may justify three checkmarks, although some educational expenses may justify four checkmarks.

Taking a cooking class or painting class may get one or two checkmarks.

A word of caution. Don't let money or the fear of money let you leave out things you love to do. Write it down, all of it. If push really came to shove and you had all the time in the world and money wasn't an issue at all, what would your days *really* look like?

Write it all down!

Are you ready to take inventory?

After you have completed this list, look at your items and check to see just how many items are on the list that cost money, versus those that are cost nothing.

I'll bet you a cup of coffee that the majority of your most cherished items don't cost a dime.

They are things like spending time with loved ones, reading a book, taking a hike or having great conversation with a good friend. You may write down a full moon hike or sitting on a bench with a friend to watch the sun rise.

Yes, you may have items like going to the movies or grabbing some dinner with a friend for which you may have placed one checkmark next to it. And very few, if any items, will have more than two checkmarks next to them.

Now that you are more clear about how little money you actually need to do the things you love, what exactly are you so worried about when it comes to money? Why do you work so hard? Do you really need to work so hard and so much?

Are you telling your wife or husband that you work so hard for them or the family? What do they say about that? If they wrote the same list, wouldn't they write down "spend more time with husband or wife?"

Sometimes all it takes is a little perspective.

Let's move on to the next part of this exercise.

Digging Deeper

Now that you have this list of things you love to do, look to see what you really want to do of the things you don't do because of time constraints versus financial constraints.

In our example we wrote down "elaborate trips around the world." Why is this person not taking elaborate trips around the world?

Identify the reason behind those things you wrote down in column three.

It's important that you identify with the "why" of each of the items in column three. Your personal reasons may be related to money but they could also be related to time constraints, family responsibilities, health related issues or because you have other obligations, such as a job.

Then ask yourself if there is a hidden agenda behind the reason why you are not doing this activity.

You may find that at first you thought you don't travel elaborately around the world because of money issues. But as you dig deeper you realize it's really because you don't want to do it alone. You want a life partner with whom to share your trip with.

Or perhaps the opposite is true. You're married but you really don't want to do this with your spouse but don't have the heart or ability to do it with the person you really want to do things with.

Get clarity!

Once you have your first level fear and then your second- and third-level fears, you will start to get clarity around the things you really want to do. And consequently your subconscious will help you come up with a plan to bring all of the things in your list to fruition.

All it takes is a little digging for the root of the weed (fear). Pull it out and plant a new seed (vision).

Let me give you an example.

For the Love of Horses

I love horses. I grew up with them, I've had them most of my life or I've been surrounded with them most of my life.

Horses are expensive. Having a horse or paying for horseback riding would definitely get four checkmarks.

My hidden agenda behind the excuse of horses costing a lot of money is that they also take a huge amount of time, dedication and commitment.

At this point in my life I have a daughter that is grown and no more pets – I'm completely free to do what I want and work from anywhere on the planet.

A few years ago I moved to Europe, moved to Italy, then Switzerland, then Sedona and as I am typing this I'm in California with an impending move overseas once again. If I had a horse none of these moves would be possible and I would be tied to a barn instead.

What started out as "money" being the reason for not having a horse turned out to be the invasion of my freedom. That's my real hidden agenda fear. At this point in my life I want nothing more than to be free to go where I want to go, for however long as I want, with whomever I want to.

Having the responsibilities of taking care of a horse would prevent my being able to do so.

Do you see how this hidden agenda business can filter through even your hobbies and passions?

Sometimes we say we don't do what we really love to do because of 'this' when the real reason is something completely different.

My love for horses is huge but my love for freedom and non-responsibility for a pet is bigger at this time in my life. Having said this, can you see how this gateway of fear just led me to the gateway of clarity?

Now that I no longer have to make excuses that I don't have a horse because of financial or time constraints and I have fessed up that the real fear here is to lose my freedom to remain mobile, I now am granted access to the gateway of clarity. It is here that I can see far and wide and my entire future is completely wide open to me.

It is from this place that I can choose to move to Europe or up North or down South or West or East – or anywhere I choose to for that matter.

Now that freedom has granted me access to a wide open road, I can make choices that are not based on wants and needs (the want and need to be around horses) but choices that are based on my real need, which is the need to remain free and unburdened with the responsibilities to take care of an animal.

I am now in a place of empowerment.

The exercises in this book are not only to discover your fears and their hidden agendas, they are also to identify your longings and their real hidden agendas. Once you discover the hidden agenda behind why you don't do what you are passionate about, the thing you long to do will no longer have a hold on you. Instead you come up with a plan to experience your passions whenever you can.

Be honest with yourself as you go through these exercises. Only with honesty will true revelations come and help the scales fall off your eyes so you can see what's really behind the gateway of fears and your passions.

On the next page I have listed some great money quotes. Enjoy!

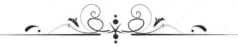

Money has never made man happy, nor will it, there is nothing in its nature to produce happiness. The more of it one has the more one wants.

Benjamin Franklin

When I was young I thought that money was the most important thing in life; now that I am old I know that it is.

Oscar Wilde

The lack of money is the root of all evil.

Mark Twain

Money won't create success, the freedom to make it will.

Nelson Mandela

Wealth is the ability to fully experience life.

Henry David Thoreau

CHAPTER 9

The Hidden Agenda Behind Questions

Facts which at first seem improbable will, even on scant explanation, drop the cloak which has hidden them and stand forth in naked and simple beauty.

Galileo Galilei

Turn Everything Into a Question

Let's look at your own gateway of clarity in more depth.

Some of the most common questions asked by almost anyone today are the following:

- Who am I?

- Why am I here?

- What is my purpose here?

- How will I get there?

- When is it over?

Or perhaps you've asked yourself simpler but still important questions such as these:

- Why am I not as successful as I thought I'd be at this time of my life?

- Why did this happen to me?

- How can I trust again after I've been hurt so much?

- Is now the right time to have a child?

- Is he or she the love of my life?

- Should I get divorced?

- Where should invest my money?

- Should I buy or rent a house?

- Should I move? Where to?

- Which job should I take?

- Should I start my own business?

Let's go over these questions one by one and see what the apparent fears are and then dig for the *hidden agenda* behind the apparent fear.

Remember, the *hidden agenda* is different for everyone and depends greatly on the type of impact the original event had on you.

In other words, the moment you were first exposed to a particular event, which made such an impression on you, that every time this event gets triggered by a form of anchor, your fear gets triggered as well.

This fear only gets perpetuated and magnified throughout other events in your life. And unless you deal with this fear once and for all, they will only continue to peek their heads out from time to time to remind you that there are still skeletons in your closed that would like to get dressed up as teddy bears, once and for all.

Let's take the more serious questions one by one to see how we can move through the gateway of fear to arrive at the gateway of clarity:

By far one of the most asked questions by humanity today is this one:

- Who am I?

It's a question that communicates lack of clarity, which means there is a fear present or the question wouldn't have to be asked in the first place. In other words, when you are asking a question in order to get clarification, it's because you are clearly not seeing the field of potential along with its answers because that gateway of clarity is still closed.

Every question you ask is a hint that there is an underlying fear that begs to be acknowledged, understood and eventually transmuted.

Go back to the gateway of fear instead of trying to find an answer to your question. When you are willing to face and master the fear, the answer to your question will be revealed to you when you come to the gateway of clarity.

Put The Focus On The Fear

So instead of asking the question "who am I" turn the question around and ask it this way:

- What fears are preventing me from seeing who I truly am?

Now the focus is off you and who you are and instead is focusing on the fear. The very fear that has its own energy that wants and needs to be acknowledged, understood and transmuted.

Find the Hidden Agenda Fear of the Question

If this is a particular question that you are asking yourself often, turn the question around and go 3-4 layers deep to find out what fears are present that hold you back from seeing the real you.

Then apply the same strategy to these questions:

- Why am I here?

- What is my purpose here?

These are amazing questions almost all people ask themselves. What is your mission? What does your higher Self want to express while you're here on this planet?

Turn the question around and instead ask:

- What fears are present that make me not see or go after my true mission and purpose?

You may come up with many first level fears, such as fear of failure, lack of funding available to do what you really want to do, lack of support, family responsibility, lack of time, and so on. All of which are excuses, all be it valid excuses, but excuses nonetheless.

Remember, to dig for the *hidden agenda fear*. That's where the real culprit lies in helping you get to the gateway of clarity.

Here is another question many people ask themselves.

- How will I get there?

Here you are, you know your mission, you know exactly what you want, but you can't see how you can get there and give birth to your amazing dream. Remember that the real question is not "how will you get there" but the real question is:

- What fears are present that prevent me from realizing my dreams?

Again, here you may come up with another slew of level one fears, such as lack of time, lack of support, lack of money, lack of know-how. These are all just excuses, no matter how valid they are.

You must know that when you are truly about your highest calling, everything you need to realize your dream will be present and there for the taking. This includes money, support, a business plan, the location, the material or employees, including the clients and the love of your life.

If you are standing in the field of clarity then you know this and you stop worrying.

If you're worried or complaining that the help is not there or the money is not there and that life is so hard and things move so slowly, then the door to gateway two has not yet been opened to you. Go back to gateway one and face and master your fears first.

And the last question I hear often from people is this one:

- When is it over?

Clearly this is a question from people who are tired of life. They are tired of the rat race or tired of not having achieved what they were hoping or desiring to achieve, and they just want life to end and be done with it already.

Instead of asking "when is it over," why not ask it while standing in front of the gateway of fear?

- What fears are preventing me from enjoying life to the fullest?

This is a question that only you can answer.

From my own consulting work with high profile people let me assure you that everyone has asked themselves at one point or another, why life is not as full as they would like it to be.

I'm a trained grief and suicide hotline counselor and the number one candidate to committing suicide are white males in their fifties and sixties. Why?

Because many of them see themselves as failures. Perhaps their health is declining or they've lost everything in a business failure or a divorce. They also know that life is heading towards its end and they feel unaccomplished. They lose hope.

They wonder, why give a damn and work so hard when it's going to be over soon anyways?

There are countless people on this planet who have plenty of money and support and friends and opportunities, and yet their life seems to be missing something.

And there are plenty of people who don't have enough money who constantly blame their circumstances about not being able to live their highest expression.

Both, the poor and the wealthy, are often finding themselves in the exact same position: in front of the gateway of clarity, wondering why they can't force that gateway open to see what's missing in their life.

What's missing when you seek clarity is always the same thing: a fear has been left unresolved in the past (related to this very issue of clarity that you are seeking a solution for). And until and unless you are willing to take a step back and face your fears and then transform your fear so it loses its electric charge, you will not be able to get to this gateway of clarity, where all things become so much more transparent.

Exercise: Find Their Fears

Let's look at these questions begging for clarity and see which ones apply to you.

Take out your workbook and write down some of the questions you have about life. See the next page for some examples.

For each of these questions find your first-, second-, third- and fourth level fears associated with the question.

Remember to turn your question around to locating the fear that is related to the question you are seeking clarity for. Keep asking 'why' and 'so what' questions until you find the real fear, the *hidden agenda fear*.

- Why am I not as successful as I thought I'd be at this time of my life?

- Why did this happen to me?

- How can I trust again after I've been hurt so much?

- Is now the right time to have a child?

- Is he or she the love of my life?

- Should I get divorced?

- Where should invest my money?

- Should I buy or rent a house?

- Should I move? Where to?

- Which job should I take?

- Should I start my own business?

- Should I hire this employee?

- Is this the right contractor for the job?

Once you have come face to face with the hidden agenda of the fears related to all of your clarity-seeking questions, you will need to come up with a tactical plan to turn your fear into a joy, or at minimum into a situation where the event no longer has an energetic hold on you.

This may mean creating active steps to creating an opposite scenario. For example, your question of clarity may be why you haven't found true love yet even though you're already 40 years old.

Your initial fear is that finding a loved one may then rob you of your freedom, which you now enjoy so much.

Your hidden agenda fear, however, may be that you are terrified of falling madly in love only to see your new mate cheat on you, just like your mother cheated on your dad and left the family to be with her new lover. The real hidden agenda fear is *abandonment*.

Next, you will actively work on transmuting this fear. You may have to see a therapist and find outside help for your specific issue.

You may find the courage to discuss this issue directly with your mom and get her side of the story. You may find that her story is valid, that she had good reasons for her stepping out on your dad and that you may find a new appreciation for why she did what she did.

You may also talk to your dad and see what his viewpoint is about this whole thing.

Who knows? You won't know the full truth until you ask for the whole truth.

Remember Bruce Lee's wisdom:

"The usefulness of a cup is its emptiness."

When it comes to your fears, be without judgment even you remember the anchor that first triggered it in your life.

Your whole goal here is to acknowledge and understand your fear and then work with it to turn it around into a brand new, positive and beneficial energy that will serve you.

As you show interest in wanting to resolve these fears and you take active steps to do so, the Universe will come towards you in the most amazing ways. Don't underestimate the power of taking your first step.

Lao Russell once spoke these wise words:

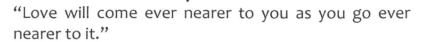

"Love will come ever nearer to you as you go ever nearer to it."

Fear works the same way. Fear wants to be resolved too. Go ever nearer to it, face it, and then watch it transform into something beautiful right before you.

The time to take the ostrich approach and keep your head in the sand pretending the fear doesn't exist is not going to resolve anything and it's certainly not going to help those fears get transmuted.

The fears will only pop their heads out from time to time, different people, different circumstances, same lessons – in an effort for you to look these fears in the eye.

As you work with one fear and one issue of clarity, you will notice that all kinds of other issues crop up that you didn't even know were there.

Don't fret about these issues, take them as they come and know that they are here to be validated and worked on just like all your other fears.

As you commit to yourself to learning and growing more about your magnificence, the faster this energy of healing is going to coil and speed up and produce positive results for you.

While you are reading this book you have perhaps already spent several hours or days working on your fears and getting more clear with what you want.

Soon these steps become second nature to you and you will be able to spot the hidden agenda within just a few seconds, without ever having to take notes.

This happens almost automatically. You find yourself asking a question and your subconscious percolates to your conscience saying:

> "Hey, that's a question seeking clarity. Let me turn this question around."

You then turn the question of clarity around because you know the only reason you are seeking clarity is because here is an underlying fear that is preventing you from opening the gateway of clarity in the first place.

You then see your first fear and immediately pick up on the second and third fear and quickly find the hidden agenda fear.

From here you will have one 'aha' moment after another. You will quickly see how things are linked to events of the past, things you have long forgotten and most likely shoved under the rug. From here you can choose to clean house and resolve these ancient energies so that you can move forward with a crystal clear knowing what steps to take next.

The gateway of clarity is like standing on top of the Jungfrau Joch Mountain in the Swiss Alps on a beautiful sunny day. The mighty Jungfrau sits at 11,388 feet (3,471 meters) on a sunny day, you can see well into Italy, over to France and up North towards the rest of the country.

From the gateway of clarity you can see where you want to go, what your obstacles are and what route is the best course of action. And because you have the bird's eye view of any situation, you know how to respond with grace to each task at hand.

You don't choose things because you have to or because you're desperate, but because they are in alignment with you and serve all parties equally as well.

From this place of clarity your life can truly change and become the life where potentials can be turned into realities. From this vast place of possibilities you also know how your choices affect those around you, including yourself. You make wiser choices and refrain from making hasty decisions.

You step out of immature reactiveness and step into controlled, mature responsiveness.

You know that your choices have consequences and because you see so clearly into the future and the past (where your fears used to fester), you will make choices from a place of real power.

There is another beautiful step that takes place when you find yourself in this vast field of clarity. Help will come out of the woodwork from all angles and directions.

It's as if the entire Universe and world is here to serve and assure your every successful step. It's quite miraculous to see how much quicker you get to arrive at solutions, how much easier it is for help to show up in every way possible, whether it's financial or moral support or any other type of support to help get things done.

If you've been feeling like you're paddling up stream or that you've been pushing the river, forcing things to unfold only to find yourself frustrated along the way, you will realize that all of that excessive energy in trying to control others or situations was so unnecessary.

This field of potential and clarity is a place of calm, a place of divine proportions that allows you to see what others don't see. This field gives you the advantage in every situation.

It's as if you have a crystal ball at your disposal, without the actual crystal ball. Your intuition is heightened and your senses function at much higher and more optimal levels that give you the short cut to getting things done more efficiently and more effectively.

CHAPTER 10

The Four Gateways in Practicality

"Be practical as well as generous in your ideals. Keep your eyes on the stars, but remember to keep your feet on the ground."

Theodore Roosevelt

The Four Gateways In Practicality

I wish I could tell you that this is a one-time journey from gateway one until you reach gateway four. It is not.

What I can tell you, however, is that each turn gets easier and quicker. This is what I meant earlier when I said that 'energy coils.' When energy runs in a straight line, it keeps steady at its current rate of speed. As soon as we coil it, however, energy speeds up and gains momentum.

The same thing applies to you and this learning curve. The first time you do these exercises you may feel like you're agonizing through them. Especially since fears always tend to tug on our emotions.

If you can stick with this for a few days or a few weeks and actively resolve your fears, you will find that there is no fear on this planet that can have a hold on you.

Each journey or question starts with the gateway of fear. It is only when we have successfully walked through that gateway and faced what's behind each gateway that we are led to the next gateway.

> "How often do I have to face these gateways?" you may wonder.

It depends.

This is the first time you are presented with this protocol and it will be a most intense journey, because it's a journey inward, the shortest, yet longest journey of them all.

While you may be inclined to focus on gateways two (clarity) and three (power), I urge you to face gateway one first (fear). Follow the sequence and trust that gateways two, three and four (wisdom) will be shown to you as you do your work.

This may be harder for those of you who are power-, status- or success hungry. Do the work anyways.

Think of gateway four as the beautiful result or reward for having done the work with gateways one, two and three. This is the type of reward that no one can take away from you.

Once you start this journey, you will notice that you will probably be approached by your friends, co-workers and even strangers, who will suddenly be drawn to you because you exude a new type of energy that serves like a magnet to them. They will want to bask in your new energy, which is the elixir of your inner power and the tincture of wisdom – which all souls so desperately need.

The Gateway of Inner Power

Every time you have a question about clarity, your automatic trigger needs to guide you back to gateway number one: the gateway of fear.

What fear is there that prevents you from seeing the answer to your question clearly?

Most people, however, as they stand in front of the gateway of clarity, all they can ask is "how can I pry this door open because what I really want is power/fame/success/wealth/love."

Rather than forcing your way through this gateway of clarity, take a step back and start from the beginning: the gateway of fear.

From there you find your various layers of fears until you reach the hidden agenda fear. And then the work begins. You create active steps to overcoming that fear. Some of these fears can be resolved by a mere decision and remembrance of what triggered the fear itself. And others, like my public speaking fear, took over a year to cease having a hold on me.

Above all, you must be committed to yourself. When another fear crops up, and they will, you follow the same process. Inquire within, resolve the fear by actively working on it until you reach a level of power in that particular department.

Don't worry excessively about reaching the gateway of elder wisdom. It will happen somewhat automatically as you are dedicated to your personal development and your unfolding, and provided you don't let power get to your head once you're through the gateway of power. There is always that chance if you choose not to take your lessons learned and use that power for selfish reasons.

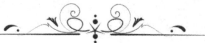

Remember how my Dad said I wouldn't amount to anything and how I dropped out of 8th grade because I felt it futile to go on?

He was not the only reason for my dropping out of school. I was also faced with a mother who demanded that I started to pay rent at home. I was only 15 years old and had a horse to take care of and already got up at 4 a.m. every day, seven days a week, and worked every Wednesday and Saturday to pay for my horse. I couldn't find a way to continue that, pay for my horse's rent, pay rent at home and go to school. It was just too much.

I had zero fear about moving out, I did have huge fear of losing my horse.

My hidden agenda fear behind losing my horse was that I would be alone. My dad had left when I was 12, I am faced with moving out and all I had left was my 'best friend,' my horse.

So my clarity at that time was crystal clear. I chose to move out to keep my horse over choosing to continue my education.

Was that a wise choice for a 15 year old to drop out of school and move away from home with a horse tagging along? Probably not but boy did it put me before the gateway of power in a jiffy. My self-esteem soared and I felt independent, like I could do anything.

This of course, was the 'false' gateway of power.

Had I not walked through the gateway of fear and gotten clarity on why I was going back to fix the holes in my educational path, such a comment would have completely derailed me.

Instead, I was able to overflow with compassion because I realized it wasn't personal towards me, his comment was personal toward himself. I maintained my place of power and answered with love and wisdom, telling him that I really enjoyed learning and that I was planning to continue learning more later on.

It would take another two years and me turning 45 years old when for the first time I heard him say:

"I'm proud of you."

It meant nothing to me to hear him say what I needed to hear when I was growing up. I had worked through my fear and there was no electric charge left.

I was indeed glad, however, that he had managed to muster up enough courage to actually make a compliment to his own daughter. I was proud of his achievement because I know it must have taken a lot for him to say so. Good for him.

A couple of weeks later he had several strokes, which messed up his short term memory, but seemed to heighten his long term memory.

He started sharing many stories of his upbringing that I had never heard before.

One of the stories he shared was about how his father told him that he would never amount to anything and was so disappointed in him that he didn't even know that he had graduated high school.

Due to the strokes my Dad had forgotten that he treated me exactly the same and it had become water under the bridge. My heart welled up with compassion for this man who had longed all his life to have a relationship with his own Dad but never got the chance to. His Dad passed away due to heart problems and he never reconciled with him.

I was in a place of power and here was my opportunity to choose wisdom. I chose to be a good daughter to him and my mother, no matter what happened in the past. To forgive is to forget.

Being a good daughter to them is my responsibility. Being good parents to me is theirs, and I'm not responsible for that part.

My Dad didn't walk through the gateways of fear to reach clarity and he certainly wasn't in an area of power or wisdom. He remained a victim and regurgitated to me what his father told him.

It was good to shower him with compassion and love and understanding. While his behavior did not heal him, the choices I made did wonders for my life and our relationship.

And in one swoosh all of those fears found complete healing.

I know if I can do it, so can you!

You may not be able to do anything about how others have treated you.
And you may not be held accountable for all the bad things that happened to you.

But you are responsible for how you react to those things.

We are not promised an easy, healthy or abundant life. We are just promised a life. What we do with it is completely up to each of us.

Do the work. Only you can do it.

I would love to hear from you and how things are going for you in this process. Please send your success stories and how this process works for you to info@corefreedom.com. I promise to read all submission but may not be individually able to respond to all.

If you want to work with me on a one-on-one basis and need help with this process, you can contact my assistant at the same email address. I work with presidents, CEOs and otherwise influential people such as government officials and celebrities. I only work with a very limited number of individuals to assure complete focus and success. To see if you qualify, visit the following address: http://corefreedom.com/consulting.

CHAPTER 11

Your Success Formula

"The most important single ingredient in the formula of success is knowing how to get along with people."

Theodore Roosevelt

Your Success Formula

Many books have been written about how to influence others, how to get along with others, how to read people and how to use it all to your advantage or to build your business with that knowledge.

Instead of spending so much time trying to figure out others, spend a fraction of that time on figuring out yourself first by applying the steps you have learned in this book. And when you do, you will realize that everyone to some degree or another, functions exactly like you:

- Everyone wants to matter and be important to at least one person

- Everyone wants to love and be loved

- Everyone wants to contribute to this world in some way or form

Everything you and anyone else ever do always has a *hidden agenda* that will bring them back to these facts.

When you get this on a soul level, life and business become easy and simple - one of servitude.

So rather than spending time figuring out others, spend time figuring out yourself. How you can serve others will become so crystal clear to you, you will wonder why you didn't see these things earlier.

To sum up this book, here is your simple formula for living your life filled with meaning and purpose:

Step 1:

Turn everything into a question.

Get in the habit of turning sentences into questions. Every question creates a void that must be filled with its equivalent answer. In other words, your intuition works 24 hours a day, 7 days a week, to finding the perfect answers to your questions.

Step 2:

Listen for the answer.

If you do not see the answer to your question, it's because there is a fear blocking your vision, because it wants to be acknowledged and resolved first.

Step 3:

Face and master your fears.

Instead of forcing the answer by getting frustrated or angry or consulting someone with a crystal ball, go back to gateway one: the gateway of fear.

Follow the steps taught in this book to get through this most important gateway!

Step 4:

Find your hidden agenda fear.

I cannot stress this step enough. Facing your 'initial' fear is one thing, facing your *hidden agenda fear* is the **key** to getting through this gateway.

Remember to not only face your fear but to master it.

Step 5:

Choose humility over arrogance.

Once you have your answers and you are crystal clear about your next steps, you will be faced with the gateway of power.

Many will fail here because they will let their status of power, accomplishments, fame, or money serve their egos, rather their soul.

Beware not to fall for false sense of power but remember that making powerful choices based on humility are the key to getting to the next gateway.

Step 6:

Choose wisdom and discernment.

Much will be shown to you when you get to this gateway, not only about yourself, but about others as well.

Remain honorable and remember that energy always flows downhill much faster than it does uphill.

In other words, the journey from gateway one to gateway four is an uphill climb, and arduous journey that most will avoid at all cost. Ego-driven people for the most part want things quickly and in big quantities, whether it's power, money or fame.

The person who has been through this gateway displays a strength of character that came at a very high cost and in turn they will protect their character at all cost. Meaning, they will not let fear stand in their way, they will not sell out and they will certainly not chase after money, people, false sense of power or illusions.

Step 7:

Rinse and repeat for each challenge or problem in your life.

These steps are not to be walked just one time and then you're done. These steps apply to each of your challenges, fears or problems.

The first time you go through these exercises you will find it agonizing, cumbersome and even frustrating. Do it anyway.

The second and third time the process will become much quicker and more pleasurable.
Especially when you get one 'aha' moment after the other and you realize that this is the key to healing old wounds.

When you make this formula your go-to formula to dealing with challenges in your life, these steps will become second nature to you and the entire process can take literally one to two minutes, instead of an entire day.

Think of it this way.

Straight Line Energy

- Energy that runs in a straight line runs at an even pace. Think of people who rarely accomplish anything and live lives on auto-pilot.

Downhill Energy

- Energy that runs downhill runs much faster. Unfortunately this also means dilution and loss of energy with a crash landing in sight. Descension is painful. Think of all the bad choices you made in life that had detrimental outcomes.

Uphill Energy

- Energy travelling uphill runs much slower. It takes strength and patience to walk the path of ascension. This is what we call "taking the high road."
From each new height one gains a brilliant new view of life and one's own power and strength of character increases immeasurably.

Coiled Energy

- Energy that coils gains amazing momentum with much power to charge any project you would like to get power for in your life.

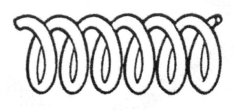

Some of the most powerful people on earth have figured out how to coil their energy and disperse its power at just the right moment.

Now create a turn and the energy will immediately speed up. Now create another turn and energy will become even faster. Think of coiling your energy to speed up the process.

That's exactly what's happening each time you are applying the formula to your four gateways!

With each step the energy speeds up and you are getting answers faster and faster. Not only about yourself but also about projects, businesses, life situations and other people.

Once again – success is assured!

The End

Thank You!

Thank you for reading this book and for playing along!

I am eager to hear your success stories. Please send me an email at info@corefreedom.com and make sure to grab your free gift at http://corefreedom.com.

List of Fears Cheat-Sheet

Physical

Dying, drowning, burning alive, falling to ones' death, getting shot, raped, attacked, attacked by an animal, ending up homeless, losing sight, hearing, paralyzed, losing a limb, becoming deaf, getting cancer or other illness, drowning, dying early, dying suddenly, accident, losing a parent, child, friend, dying before everything has been completed or accomplished, living alone, ending up alone, fear of falling, starving or being without water, fear of needles, physical abuse.

Financial

- Losing all your money or never having any of it.
- Losing your home or your retirement.
- Losing your job.
- Having your money stolen.
- Being betrayed financially or professionally or by someone you love.

Emotional

- Ending up alone.
- Being lied to.
- Having your trust broken.
- Getting cheated on.
- Emotional or verbal abuse.
- Being called name.
- Fear of not feeling understood, heard or accepted.

Mental

- Getting Alzheimer's or Dementia.
- Losing your mental faculties.
- Losing your memory.
- Becoming forgetful.
- Not recognizing friends or family.

Romance & Love

- Fear of physical intimacy.
- Emotional closeness with others.
- Fear of men or women (opposite sex).
- Fear of how to approach the opposite sex.

- Feeling confident in your gender.
- Dressing appropriately.
- Looking your best.
- Asking for a date.
- Breaking up with someone.
- Asking someone to marry you.
- Telling someone the truth.
- Getting lied to by the person you love the most.
- Having to lie to the person you love the most.
- Being left for someone else.
- Being ignored.
- Being undervalued.
- Being treated like a doormat.

Miscellaneous

- Telling the truth.
- Speaking up to defend yourself or someone else.
- Giving a compliment.
- Hiring or firing someone.
- Giving a review at work.
- Public speaking.
- Watch your parents age and die from horrible illnesses.
- Not having an education.
- Feeling inadequate.
- Self-worthiness issues/
- Fear of choosing wrong.
- Fear of ladders.

- Fear of animals, spiders, insects, snakes, mice, bats, cockroaches.

Fears for Humanity or the World

- Injustice.
- Child or elder abuse.
- Animal abuse.
- Abortion.
- Meat industry.
- Lack of water.
- Government issues.
- Weather control.
- Chemtrails.
- Conspiracy issues.
- Extra-terrestrials.
- Reptilians.
- Food or water poisoning.
- Implantable chips.
- Computerization of humanity.
- Abortion rights.
- Human trafficking.

About The Author

Cha~zay was born and raised in Switzerland. She started her career working for the Swiss Government and the Swiss Private Banking Industry. She moved to the U.S. in 1989 to learn English.

Cha~zay Sandhriel

She started a new life and career in California where she focused on building teams for European technology start-up companies settling in Silicon Valley.

A tragic event in 2006 propelled her to leave the United States where she spent 7 years mostly in silence and solitude. During this time she studied for her Ph.D.'s in Metaphysical Sciences and Holistic Life Coaching. In 2012 she moved to Sedona to write two books.

Today she spends her time as a Consciousness Consultant and Inter-Connectedness Mentor to executives, CEOs, presidents, government officials and celebrities.

Work with Dr. Cha~zay

Cha~zay works on a one-on-one basis with highly influential people such as presidents, CEOs, government officials, celebrities and other well-known public figures.

Her one-of-a-kind interconnectedness training specializes in peeling back the layers that prevent her clients from living fully and in each present moment. Working with Dr. Cha~zay ensures paradigm shifts on all levels, whether personal, professional or spiritual.

To see if you qualify for a complimentary one-hour inter-connectedness training session visit here: http://corefreedom.com/consulting.

Workshops and Speaking

Dr. Cha~zay is available to facilitate employee workshops as well as speaking engagements such as keynotes, radio, podcasts, and panel discussions. Contact her office at media@corefreedom.com with details about your event.

Testimonial

"Dr. Cha~zay is probably the most 'present' person I have ever met. Her unique ability, her gift, gives her insight and understanding that transcend traditional intuition and professional training. I am more 'awake' personally and professionally than I've ever been. I have learned more about myself and the possibilities available to me from Dr. Cha-zay than any workshop, book, individual coach or consultant I have encountered."

Dennis Thompson
Managing Partner, Thompson Associates

Contact

General: info@corefreedom.com

Media/Radio/Speaking: media@corefreedom.com

Community: http://corefreedom.com/community

Consulting: http://corefreedom.com/consulting

Podcast: http://corefreedom.com/show

Facebook: http://facebook.com/drchazay

LinkedIn: http://linkedin.com/in/corefreedom

YouTube: http://youtube.com/blueprintforlove

Other Books by Dr. Cha~zay

I am Dying, Shit! Not Again!

A book about Dr. Cha~zay's three near death experiences. Get it on Amazon.

The Limp, The Wet, The Hard – Unlocking the Mysteries of Handshakes

A book about the meaning of various handshakes and how to develop and use intuition when shaking people's hands.

Courses by Dr. Cha~zay

Basic Dowsing Course – Programming You and Your Pendulum

Coupon Code: http://corefreedom.com/basic-dowsing

"Clear and Well explained, Double Thumbs up!! I've been looking for a good course on Dowsing for some time now and at last! I found it here!! In fact Cha~zay's course exceeds all my hopes in many ways. All sections are well explained and easy to follow and AAA support is provided if you have any questions. I will be telling all my friends to get this course. If you're on the fence about whether to get the course, then get it! Believe me it's the best one out there by a mile. "

Bruce E. Hilton

Advanced Dowsing Course – Transcendental Dowsing For Success

Coupon Code: http://corefreedom.com/advanced-dowsing

"Couldn't be happier! I just completed the Advanced Dowsing Course and I am blown away at the amount of knowledge that is packed into this course! Dr. Cha Zay has taken my dowsing skills to an entirely new level. Thank you so much for this course."

Scott Graft

The Psychology of Colors – Achieve More Success with Colors

Coupon Code: http://corefreedom.com/color-psychology

*"**This is a masterpiece** of how to balance your life in colors and chakras. It is packed full of useful information for everyday life and how it all connects to your spiritual evolution as well. Cha~zay really shows her deep knowledge of metaphysics in a way anyone can understand and use."*

Guy Girard

Teleseminar Mastery Course – Create Courses With Your Telephone

Coupon Code: http: corefreedom.com/teleseminars

*"**Excellent, inspiring course!** This course has inspired me with so many ideas that my head is spinning! It is packed full of information on why and how to use teleseminars to increase business and created passive streams of income - no detail is spared!"*

Jessica Barst

"Wow, this course is fun and informative. Even though I have experience in this area, Cha~zay really simplifies the steps and creates a brilliant picture of how to succeed from anywhere with a telephone line. If I had known ALL of this years ago...it would have saved me a lot of time! The instructor presents well-structured content with a caring tone that makes the material easy to follow and absorb. Great way to leverage expertise with larger audiences and tap even greater income."

Bodhi Horne

Notes

Notes

Made in the USA
Monee, IL
21 May 2020

31613469R00098